Healing in the Whole Bible

Part Two

– Under the New Testament –

Ken Chant

Healing in the Whole Bible

Part Two

– Under the New Testament –

Ken Chant

Copyright © 2012 Ken Chant

ISBN 978-1-61529-062-8

For information on reordering contact:

Vision Publishing
1672 Main St. E 109
Ramona, CA 92065
1-800-9-VISION
www.booksbyvision.com

A NOTE ON GENDER

It is unfortunate that the English language does not contain an adequate generic pronoun (especially in the singular number) that includes without bias both male and female. So *"he, him, his, man, mankind,"* with their plurals, must do the work for both sexes. Accordingly, wherever it is appropriate to do so in the following pages, please include the feminine gender in the masculine, and vice versa.

FOOTNOTES

A work once fully referenced will thereafter be noted either by "ibid" or "op. cit."

Whoever thinks a faultless Piece to see,
Thinks what ne'er was, nor is, nor e'er shall be.
In every Work, regard the *Writer's End*,
Since none can compass more than they *Intend*;
And if the *Means* be just, the *Conduct* true,
Applause, in spite of trivial Faults, is due . . .
Most Criticks, fond of some subservient Art,
Still make the *Whole* depend upon a *Part*,
They talk of *Principle*, but *Notions* prize,
And All to one lov'd Folly Sacrifice.

. . . .

Good-Nature and *Good-Sense* must ever join;
To Err is* Human; *to Forgive, Divine. [1]

---

(1) "Criticks" and "Humane" were the 17th-century spellings of "critics" and "human". Alexander Pope, <u>An Essay on Criticism</u> (1711), lines 253-266, 524-525.

Contents

Miracles in the Acts of the Apostles – the word of God confirmed by "signs, wonders, and miracles".

Faith in the name of Jesus – our true wealth – our true power – our true faith – salvation and healing by the Name – going in his name to heal the sick and cast out demons.

A man delivered to Satan – around the Table of the Lord – why the Corinthians were sick – discerning the *"body of Christ"* – a holy table – the judgment of God – how to receive healing at the Lord's Table – the supernatural *"gift of healing"*.

Paul at Corinth and in Galatia – a messenger of Satan – was Paul sickly and nearly blind? – his *"big letter(s)´*?

Epaphroditus, Timothy, and Trophimus – Paul's great prayer for the Thessalonicans – the chastening of the Father.

The use of the word *"better"* in Hebrews – what it means to *"call for the elders of the church"* – can you also call the physician? – the healing covenant in *James 5:14-15* – life, love, and many days – more reasons to accept the healing covenant: God's mighty promises; the promise of prosperity; various references – divine healing in prophecy: the words of Joel; false Christs and false signs; healing in the millennium; conclusion.

God's eternal promise of good health – more reasons to believe –divine healing in prophecy and in the millennium – conclusion.

ABBREVIATIONS

Abbreviations commonly used for the books of the Bible are

Genesis	Ge	Habakkuk	Hb
Exodus	Ex	Zephaniah	Zp
Leviticus	Le	Haggai	Hg
Numbers	Nu	Zechariah	Zc
Deuteronomy	De	Malachi	Mal
Joshua	Js		
Judges	Jg		
Ruth	Ru	Matthew	Mt
1 Samuel	1 Sa	Mark	Mk
2 Samuel	2 Sa	Luke	Lu
1 Kings	1 Kg	John	Jn
2 Kings	2 Kg	Acts	Ac
1 Chronicles	1 Ch	Romans	Ro
2 Chronicles	2 Ch	1 Corinthians	1 Co
Ezra	Ezr	2 Corinthians	2 Co
Nehemiah	Ne	Galatians	Ga
Esther	Es	Ephesians	Ep
Job	Jb	Philippians	Ph
Psalm	Ps	Colossians	Cl
Proverbs	Pr	1 Thessalonians	1 Th
Ecclesiastes	Ec	2 Thessalonians	2 Th
Song of Songs	Ca *	1 Timothy	1 Ti
Isaiah	Is	2 Timothy	2 Ti
Jeremiah	Je	Titus	Tit
Lamentations	La	Philemon	Phm
Ezekiel	Ez	Hebrews	He
Daniel	Da	James	Ja
Hosea	Ho	1 Peter	1 Pe
Joel	Jl	2 Peter	2 Pe
Amos	Am	1 John	1 Jn
Obadiah	Ob	2 John	2 Jn
Jonah	Jo	3 John	3 Jn
Micah	Mi	Jude	Ju
Nahum	Na	Revelation	Re

Ca is an abbreviation of *Canticles*, a derivative of the Latin name of the *Song of Solomon*, which is sometimes also called the *Song of Songs*.

THE BOOK NO-ONE READS!

This book is the second of two volumes dealing with the theme of *Healing in the Whole Bible*. The first volume studied the healing covenant in the *Old Testament*, while this explores the position of the healing covenant in the *New Testament*.

Here is sacred territory indeed!

I tremble before the very title of the great Book upon which this lesser study is based: *The New Testament of our Lord and Saviour Jesus Christ.* [2] How can anyone faithfully reveal the height and depth of the glorious revelation of Christ contained in those Spirit-inbreathed gospels and letters? I have read right through the *New Testament* probably 40 times and devoted additional thousands of hours to meticulous study of almost every part of it. Yet in the end I must agree with Henry David Thoreau, who once declared that no-one has *ever* truly *read* (let alone understood) the teaching of Jesus and the apostles –

> It is remarkable that, notwithstanding the universal favour with which the *New Testament* is outwardly received, and even the bigotry with which it is defended, there is no hospitality shown to, there is no appreciation of, the order of truth with which it deals. I know of no book that has so few readers. There is none so truly strange, heretical, and unpopular. To Christians, no less than Greeks and Jews, it is foolishness and a stumbling-block. There are, indeed, severe things in it which no man should read aloud more than once –
>
> *Seek first the kingdom of heaven . . . Lay not up for yourselves treasures on earth . . . If thou wilt be perfect,*

---

(2) This was the name it bore for many centuries in all printed Bibles. Our more prosaic, and less reverential custom, is simply to use the title *The New Testament.*

go and sell that thou hast, and give to the poor, and thou shalt have treasure in heaven . . . For what is a man profited if he shall gain the whole world, and lose his own soul? Or what shall a man give in exchange for his soul?

Think of the Yankees! –

Verily, I say unto you, if ye have faith as a grain of mustard seed, ye shall say unto this mountain, Remove hence to yonder place, and it shall remove; and nothing shall be impossible unto you.

Think of repeating these things to a New England audience! . . . Who, without cant, can read them aloud? Who, without cant, can hear them and not go out of the meeting-house? They never *were* read, they never *were* heard. Let but one of these sentences be rightly read, from any pulpit in the land, and there would not be left one stone of that meeting-house upon another! [3]

One cannot help but feel the humiliating truth of those words. Yet, despite the impossibility of truly representing, without error, the message of the *New Testament*, the attempt must be made. Much dirt comes up with the gold, but the value of the treasure gained is worth the toil and the soil.

I must suppose then that the following pages contain fact that is inescapably mixed with folly. Yet I can but strive to keep the bright light of divine truth as little shadowed by fault as human frailty will allow. This much at least is certain: the healing covenant God has made with his church is fraught with many mysteries. Some scholars reject the very idea of such a covenant. Others accept it too glibly, and, like the proverbial ostrich, bury their heads in the sand of a refusal to face problems (*"why are some not healed . . . why do unbelievers often gain healing more readily than committed believers . . . why do some miracles not last" . . . and the like*). This book tries to steer a more middle path –

---

(3) <u>A Week on the Concord and Merrimack Rivers</u> (first published in 1849); The Heritage Press, Norwalk CT, 1975; pg. 57-58 ("Sunday").

on the one hand to affirm the covenant as strongly as possible; but on the other, to acknowledge that at best, here as everywhere, we can never advance beyond seeing fragments of the truth *"through a piece of dark glass"* (1 Co 13:12).

So then, for such stumbles as you may discover, I plead for the mercy that Alexander Pope, in the lines quoted a few pages back, urged upon all readers. If I have not achieved all that I had hoped, at least (as the poet said) my intentions were good, the means were just, and my conduct true. So perhaps, despite some "trivial faults" this book may merit at least a little applause!

CHAPTER ONE:

JESUS THE HEALER

See the wretch that long has tossed
On the thorny bed of pain
At length repair his vigour lost,
And breathe and walk again.:
The meanest floweret of the vale,
The simplest note that swells the gale,
The common sun, the air, the skies,
To him are opening Paradise. [4]

I f the revelation of God as *Yahweh-Rapha* (The-Lord-Your-Healer) was a significant part of the old covenant, [5] it is even more so of the new. Beginning with the four gospels and the ministry of Jesus, healing the sick holds a prominent place in the history of early church –

Let us begin with a simple analysis of the healing ministry of Jesus, based upon the story told in the four gospels. Immediately it becomes evident that Christ gave substantial time and effort to encourage sick people to embrace God's ancient healing covenant –

THE MIRACLES OF JESUS

1) Five hundred verses, equal to fourteen average chapters, are devoted to his healing ministry – far more space than is given to any other subject or event.

---

(4) Thomas Gray (1716-1761), <u>Vicissitude</u>.

(5) See the book that is both precursor and partner to this one, my book, <u>Healing in the Whole Bible – Under the Old Covenant</u>.

2) There are more than fifteen accounts of the Lord healing great crowds – literally thousands of miracles of healing and deliverance took place during the three years of his public ministry.

3) At least thirty individual miracles of healing are described.

4) Here are the references to the healing ministry of Jesus –

MULTITUDES HEALED

Mt 4:23-24; 8:16-17; 9:35; 11:5; 12:15; 14:14; 14:34-36; 15:30-31; 19:2; 21:14; Mk 1:32-34; 1:39; 3:10-11; 6:54-56; Lu 4:40-41; 5:15; 6:17-19; 7:21-23; 9:11; Jn 2:23; 6:2; 7:31.

SPECIFIC MIRACLES OF HEALING

A leper	Mt 8:1-3
Centurion's servant	Mt 8:5-13; Lu 7:1-10
Peter's mother-in-law	Mt 8:14-15; Mk 1:30-31; Lu 4:38-39
Two demoniacs	Mt 8:28-34; Mk 5:1-20; Lu 4:38-39
Paralysed man	Mt 9:1-8; Mk 2:1-12; Lu 5:18-26
Ruler's daughter	Mt 9:18-19, 23-26; Mk 5:22-24,35-43; Lu 8:41-56.
Woman with issue of blood	Mt 9:20-22; Mk 5:25-34;Lu 8:43-48
Two blind men	Mt 9:27-31
Dumb man	Mt 9:32-33
Man with withered hand	Mt 12:10-13; Mk 3:1-5; Lu 6:6-10
Blind and dumb demoniac	Mt 12:22-23
People at Nazareth	Mt 13:58
Daughter of Canaanite woman	Mt 5:21-28; Mk. 7:24-30
Lunatic boy	Mt 17:14-21; Mk 9:14-29; Lu 9:37-42
Two blind men	Mt 20:30-34
Demoniac	Mk 1:23-28; Lu 4:33-37
Leper	Mk 1:40-45; Lu 5:12-14
Deaf and dumb man	Mk 7:31-37
Blind man	Mk 8:22-26

Bartimaeus...................................... Mk 10:46-52; Lu 18:35-43

Widow of Nain .... Lk 7:11-16

Mary Magdalene .... Lu 8:2

Demoniac .... Lu 11:14

Crippled woman .... Lu 13:11-17

Man with dropsy .... Lu 14:1-6

Ten lepers .... Lu 17:11-19

Malchus .... Lu 22:51

Nobleman's son .... Jn 4:46-54

Cripple at Bethesda .... Jn 5:1-19

Blind man .... Jn 9:1-7

Lazarus .... Jn 11:1-46

OTHER MIRACLES AND WONDERS

The storm hushed .... Mt 8:26; Mk 4:39; Lu 8:24

Feeding a multitude .... Mt 14:15; 15:32; Mk 6:41; 8:8; Lu 9:12; Jn 6:5

Walking on the sea .... Mt 14:25; Mk 6:49; Jn 6:19

Tribute money obtained .... Mt 17:24

Cursing the fig tree .... Mt 21:19

Amazing fish catch .... Lu 5:6; Jn 21:6

Water changed to wine .... Jn 2:9

Escape from the crowd .... Lu 4:29-30; Jn 8:59; 10:39; 18:6

Many raised from the dead .... Mt 27:52-53

The transfiguration .... Mt 17:2; Mk 9:2; Lu 9:29

MANY OTHER SIGNS

John summarises the incredible healing ministry of Christ by saying –

> *Jesus performed many other miracles that his disciples personally witnessed, although they are not described in this book. But the ones that are written here, are*

recorded so that you may believe that Jesus is the Christ, the Son of God, and that believing you may find life in his name . . . There are many other things that Jesus did; so many, that if all of them were to be written, I suppose the world itself could not contain the books that would be needed! (Jn 20:30-31; 21:25).

Remember, this was all accomplished in the space of probably less than three years of public ministry. The physical and mental energy of the Lord is amazing! No wonder the apostle Peter cried out to the crowd in Jerusalem: *"Jesus of Nazareth was a man attested to you by God with mighty miracles and wonders and signs, which God did through him in your midst!"* (Ac 2:22).

Indisputably, the Lord Jesus Christ demonstrated that to him belonged the covenant name *JAHWEH-RAPHA*. Beyond doubt he showed himself to be *"The-Lord-Your-Healer"*, the Great Physician of his people!

WHY CHRIST HEALED THE SICK

Why did Jesus heal the sick? Why did he devote so much of his limited time to this one area of human need? With only three years of public ministry before him we might have expected Christ to concentrate solely on teaching the people, especially his disciples. Instead, when the time came for him to go to Jerusalem and there to die, his disciples were still quite ignorant about the real identity of their Lord and the real purpose of his mission (see Mk. 9:30-37; Lu. 9:51-56; 18:31-34; 24:17-21,25-26). Yet despite an urgent need to teach his disciples, Jesus allowed himself to be constantly pressed by the crowd, and he gave himself unsparingly to the ministry of healing (Mk 3:10; 5:24; 6:30-34; 7:24).

If we can find out why Jesus poured so much of himself into his healing ministry we will then have a sound basis on which to decide whether he is still offering himself to the sick as the Great Physician. That is the theme of the next chapter.

CHAPTER TWO:

WHY CHRIST HEALED THE SICK

Farewell, Life! my senses swim;
And the world is growing dim:
The thronging shadows cloud the light,
Like the advent of the night, –
Colder, colder, colder still
Upward steals a vapour chill –
Strong the earthy odour grows –
I smell the Mould above the Rose!

Welcome, Life! the Spirit strives!
Strength returns, and hope revives;
Cloudy fears and shapes forlorn
Fly like shadows at the morn, –
O'er the earth there comes a bloom –
Sunny light for sullen gloom,
Warm perfume for vapour cold,
I smell the Rose above the Mould! [6]

A search of the gospels quickly shows several major reasons why Jesus allowed the healing ministry to occupy so much his limited time. Jesus healed the sick –

TO PROVE THAT HE WAS THE MESSIAH

Eight hundred years before the Saviour's birth the prophet Isaiah predicted that when Christ came he would bring deliverance to the

---

(6) Thomas Hood (1799-1845), Farewell Life!

captives and set the prisoners free (Is 61:1). Christ quoted that prophecy at the beginning of his ministry and claimed it was fulfilled in him (Lu 4:14-21). Then he proved it by going in the power of the Holy Spirit to preach the gospel and to heal the sick. People acknowledged that his mighty works showed he was the Messiah (Jn 1:41; 6:14; 7:31; see also 10:23-25). Read also *Luke 7:16-22.*

Jesus believed that his miracles were more than sufficient to prove that he was not just *"a great prophet"* but that he was actually *"he who was to come"*, the Messiah of Israel.

Notice how the Lord was not content just to tell John about the miracles he had wrought yesterday and the day before. Far from it! The scripture says, *"in that same hour he cured many sick people of a variety of diseases, cast out many evil spirits, and restored sight to many who were blind!"* This immediate demonstration of his healing power served a double purpose –

> ***First***, it confirmed his identity as the Messiah, and revealed his willingness to provide continual up-to-date proof of that identity.

The mighty things God is still doing today through Christ serve the same purpose. Yet it must be admitted that such a demonstration is not absolutely necessary. If the miracles of Christ were wrought merely as signs of his power and true identity then one sequence of such miracles, wrought in a public place and attested by reliable witnesses would be sufficient. There would be no need for a continual repetition of the evidence.

In fact, the real and ultimate proof of Christ's identity is his resurrection from the dead, an event that cannot be repeated. We are completely dependent on the testimony of eyewitnesses for its validity. But that is true of any event separated from us by time or distance. It is absurd to say, "I will believe nothing unless I have personally seen or experienced it!" So it must also be admitted that –

> ***Second***, this demonstration of healing that Christ gave so immediately to John's emissaries was not so much a *sign of his identity* as a *mark of his compassion.*

If you doubt that, notice how John's disciples saw Jesus cure *"disease, plague, demon possession, and blindness"*; yet Christ bade them tell

John not only what they had seen, but also what they had *"heard"* – that *"the lame walk, lepers are cleansed, the deaf hear, the dead are raised up."* At least some of those miracles were not witnessed by John's disciples – they had to depend on the testimony of others for proof that such things had actually happened.

In other words, Jesus healed people in the presence of John's emissaries simply because the people were there and they were sick. He would have healed them whether or not other observers had been present to witness the fact.

So I conclude that while the healing ministry of Christ did provide contemporary proof of his Messianic identity, that proof in itself does not establish his willingness to heal the sick today. We must look further, and when we do, we observe in Jesus a degree of willingness (indeed eagerness) to bring healing to the sick that indicates a more fundamental motivation: *it is his very nature to heal.* Thus the continuation of his healing ministry today may have the same twofold impact on us as it did on the disciples of John: it shows his identity as *Messiah*; but even more, it shows his nature as *Great Physician.*

TO PROVE THAT HE WAS THE SON OF GOD

See *John 10:36-38.*

TO PROVE THAT HE WAS SENT BY GOD

John 5:36; 14:10-11.

On the day of Pentecost the apostle Peter boldly declared that the great signs and wonders wrought by the Lord Jesus Christ plainly proved he was sent by God (Ac 2:22). But Peter didn't stop there. He went on to present a still more convincing proof that Jesus was at that moment reigning in glory: he pointed to the miracle of the *outpouring of the Holy Spirit*, which the people could *"hear and see"* even while he was speaking (vs 33). But then, a short time later, none of those proofs could compare with the miracles that were occurring every day – see 3:14-16; 5:12-14; etc.

The disciples obviously followed the pattern Jesus himself had established

- they pointed to his past miracles as proof he had been sent by God
- they pointed to his present miracles (wrought through the church) as confirmation of their testimony about Christ
- and they continually expected their Lord to heal the sick in support of his claim to be *"The-Lord-Your-Healer"*.

TO PROVE THAT HEALING IS IN THE
VERY NATURE OF GOD

Christ claimed often that all the things he did were *"the works of his Father"* (Jn 5:26; 10:37-38; 14:10-11; etc). Yet the scriptures assert that God cannot change (Ps 33:11; 102:27 Ma 3:6; He 1:12; 13:8; Ja 1:17.) Therefore, if healing the sick was the proper work of God in the time of the gospels, it must still be his proper work.

Furthermore, a man's work reveals his nature – what he does describes him more clearly than any word he can speak. So too the works of God, in Christ, and in the disciples, and in faithful believers today, show very plainly that *healing the sick is in the very heart of God.*

TO FULFIL BIBLE PROPHECY

Matthew plainly states that Jesus healed the sick in express fulfilment of the oracle of Isaiah –

> *He) healed all who were sick . . . to fulfil what was spoken by the prophet Isaiah, "He took our infirmities and bore our diseases." (Mt 8:16-17; and cp. Is 53:4).*

But that prophecy refers not only to the time of Jesus' ministry in Palestine, it covers also the entire Christian era, it speaks to every generation. Is it true that we can still claim *pardon* and *peace* on the basis of the words *"he was wounded for our trangressions"* (Is 53:5)? Then this must be equally true: <u>we can still claim healing on the basis of the words,</u> *"he has borne away our sicknesses and carried away our pains . . . and through his scars we are healed"* (vs 4-5).

TO BRING GLORY TO GOD

Matthew 15:30-31.

The result of the healing ministry of Christ is plainly declared: *"They glorified God!"* Does that mean God cannot be glorified in sickness? No, for the purposes of God, and his higher praise, are indeed sometimes worked out through pain and suffering. [7] But for most practical purposes it must surely be said that God is glorified more in his people's wellbeing than he is in their illness. [8]

Even in cases similar to Job (who was taught to glorify God despite his afflictions), the *"true end"* of the Lord must be seen in deliverance. Few people can stand at the bed of a friend dying in the agony of cancer and sing joyful praises to God. But let that dread disease be driven out by the power of Christ, and see then what gladness there will be, and how greatly the Lord is glorified!

At any rate, the writers of the NT did not hesitate to record this fact, and to emphasise it: the result of the healing ministry of Christ and of the early church was to elicit from the people spontaneous and enthusiastic praise. I do not know of any place in the scripture that commends disease as a cause for thanking God, whereas good health is often noted as producing praise.

TO CONFIRM HIS WORD

Nicodemus, the educated Pharisee, said to Jesus, *"Rabbi, we know that you are a teacher sent to us by God; for no one could perform such miracles unless God were with him"* (Jn 3:2). The healing power of Christ had convincingly established his teaching as true.

Today also the Lord is willing to *"confirm (our) preaching by the miracles that attend it"* (Mk 16:20). Not that miracles by themselves are

---

(7) This subject is treated more extensively in the companion to this book, <u>Healing in the Whole Bible – *Old Testament*</u>.

(8) Do note that I am <u>not</u> saying that sickness itself glorifies God, only that God can be glorified through or despite sickness. Disease does not and cannot glorify the Father; it is a curse from which Christ came to redeem us.

sufficient proof that a man or a message is from God (cp. Mt 7:21-23); but in partnership with other factors they do have a certifying value.

Absence of the healing power of God from a church may presage a decline into lifeless orthodoxy, a mere observance of the forms of religion. But the presence of the power of God to heal keeps alive among the people a dynamic faith, an awe of the scriptures, a throbbing awareness that Christ is in his church. Paul hints at those things when he writes,

> *Stay away from those who hold a form of religion but deny its power! (2 Ti 3:5).*

TO CONFIRM HIS MINISTRY

Matthew 12:22-23.

Christ states a general principle in that passage: a person can cast out demons and bring healing to the blind and dumb only by *"the Spirit of God"*. He thrust this claim against the Pharisees, when they accused him of exorcising spirits by the power of *"the prince of demons"*. Then he pressed the point home with dry sarcasm: *"If I cast out demons by Beelzebub, by whom do your disciples cast them out?"*

The Pharisees wilted beneath his barb, because they knew full well that neither they nor their acolytes had ever brought deliverance to so much as one oppressed person.

With indisputable logic Jesus then built his argument against the Pharisees –

- he insisted that healing the sick, and especially casting out demons, could only be the work of God

- he declared that such a ministry showed the anointing of the Holy Spirit, and that God was working in his Word

- he stated that the very essence of the kingdom, and its real authority and strength, was demonstrated by this ministry

- he ruled that only those who shared with him in this work were truly his fellow-labourers

- he gave a solemn warning against ascribing the works of God to the power of Satan, for this, he said, was blasphemy against the

Holy Ghost, and would harden a person into unalterable rebellion against God.

Then in a final word, the Lord stated that good works such as healing the sick and casting out demons could not come from an *"evil tree"* – rather, they were proof of a genuine ministry and showed the handiwork of God.

However, as I have already shown, the *"tree"* must bear more than merely the fruit of healing – every other part of it must be consistent with the scriptures and the revealed will of God. There are false prophets and miracle-mongers gone out into the world to deceive the unwary (Mt 7:21-23; 24:24-25; and cp. De 13:1-3), against whom we must remain on guard.

BECAUSE HEALING IS THE "CHILDREN'S BREAD"

Mark 7:27.

Jesus obviously considered that the people of God had the same right to claim *divine healing* as children have to claim *daily bread* from their parents. This passage shows us also that the phrase in the Lord's prayer, *"Give us today our daily bread,"* may refer not only to the provision of our spiritual and physical needs, but also to *bodily healing.* Each day we should confidently expect the Lord to meet every need in this way.

BECAUSE HEALING WAS HIS PROPER WORK

Many times Christ ran foul of the Pharisees because he healed on the Sabbath day (Mt 12:9-14; Mk 3:1-6; Lu 13:10-16; 14:1-6; Jn 5:8-16; 7:23-24; 9:13-16). They hated him for despising their law, and sought to kill him. But the Lord's answer was simple and obvious –

HE PLEADED THE CAUSE OF SIMPLE HUMANITY

If an animal were trapped in a pit on the Sabbath the most zealous Pharisee would not leave it there to die. Sabbath or not, he would make every effort to rescue the beast. How much more noble must it then be, to rescue a man or woman trapped in sickness! But they only stared back in malicious silence. And the scripture says that Jesus was greatly angered by their hard-heartedness.

That incident is a vivid revelation of the Lord's attitude toward disease: he saw it as an imprisoning curse. It is as bad for a person to be gripped by infirmity as for an ox to be trapped in a pit.

Still further, the Lord challenged the Pharisees: *"Do you not loose your ox or your ass from the stall, and water and feed him on the Sabbath day?"* So also the people of God have a right to be made whole – it is their proper due, as necessary to them as food and water to the ox.

HE ACCUSED THEM OF HYPOCRISY

With deep indignation the Lord rebuked their hypocrisy. They were so bound up with obstinate and proud tradition that they had lost compassion for the suffering of the people. He was *"grieved at their hardness of heart"*. I wonder how sorrowful the Lord must feel at the lack of faith in the healing covenant that exists in many places in the church today?

HE INSISTED THAT GOD WORKS ON THE SABBATH

When they sought to kill him because he healed on the Sabbath, Jesus answered them, *"My Father is working still, and I work"* (Jn 5:17). It cannot be denied, God is constantly at work upholding and guiding the vast universe, along with the earth and all that is in it. Nor has the Father changed. His work today is identical to his work two thousand years ago.

In the same way, it cannot be denied that the work of Jesus back in the days of the Pharisees was pre-eminently one of healing the sick – in spirit, soul, and body. He considered this work to be as natural and necessary to him as the work of universal maintenance was to the Father.

Therefore, we must further insist that just as the natural work of the eternal Father has remained unchanged, so has the natural work of the eternal Son. As long as the universe needs to be upheld and directed, the Father will maintain it! As long as men and women need healing, the Son will deliver them!

BECAUSE THE PEOPLE WERE SICK

Here is a simple and beautiful phrase from the gospel of *Luke*: *"Jesus cured everyone who was in need of healing"* (9:11).

There we are plainly told that *human need* was the motivation behind Jesus' healing ministry. Simply because they were sick, he healed them.

It is difficult not to believe the same principle applies today. People are the same in their *need*; Christ is the same in his *nature*. Surely if people today come to Christ in their need, as they did in Bible days, they will discover in him the same natural willingness to receive them and to heal them?

I think the real burden of proof lies upon those who argue to the contrary. If the witness of scripture is taken at face value, then it is much easier to prove that Christ is still the healer than to show that he no longer wants to make people well.

BECAUSE HE HAD COMPASSION

I have placed this reason last because it seems to me to be the greatest. Again and again we read that the Lord Jesus Christ was moved to heal the sick because of his overwhelming love and compassion. He could not be indifferent to human suffering. He could not remain unmoved in the face of human need. Let these arresting statements provide their own conviction –

> *When Jesus saw the crowds, he had compassion for them, because they were harassed and helpless . . . and he went about all the cities and villages, teaching in their synagogues and preaching the gospel of the kingdom, and healing every disease and every infirmity (Mt 9:36-35) . . . He saw a great throng; and he had compassion on them, and healed their sick (Mt 14:14) . . . Jesus in pity touched their eyes, and immediately they received their sight (Mt 20:34) . . . Moved with pity, Jesus stretched out his hand and touched him (Mk 1:41).*

Stirred by that same compassion he also raised the dead (Lu 7:13).

Observe also the several occasions when people approached Christ and urged him to bring them healing simply on the grounds of compassion (Mt 20:30,31; Mk 9:22; 10:47-48; Lu 17:13; 18:38,39). Clearly they assumed, once they had recognised his power to heal, and that he was a man of God, that they had every right to expect him to display mercy and to cure them. To have the ability to do good but fail to do it is hardly the mark of a man of God. So they laid a claim against him on the basis of his power and the compassion he could be expected to have, and their claim was accepted. Is there any reason why we cannot do the same?

The scriptures show that God is full of compassion (Ps 86:15; 111:4; 112:4; 145:8,9). Jesus came to confirm the scriptures (including those texts) and more perfectly to reveal the Father. In this case he displayed the quality of God's compassion by healing the sick and casting out demons (Mk 5:19). Could the compassion of God be less today than it was then? Could the nature of his compassion have changed? Could he who was once moved to heal sick people by the depth of his compassion for them be no longer so moved?

I for one am constrained to believe that the Father is still moved by this same compassion, and that those who choose to do so can still reach out the hand of faith, touch him, and be made whole (Mt 14:36).

CONCLUSION

I have suggested twelve reasons why Jesus healed the sick. There may be others, but those twelve will suffice. But here is the most significant aspect of this entire chapter: with the possible exception of the first two, those reasons are just as applicable today as they were then. If Christ was constrained by such pleas to act then as Healer, it is reasonable to suppose that he will respond in the same way now. He is still *"The-Lord-your-Healer"*.

CHAPTER THREE:

A RELUCTANT HEALER?

In the hour of my distress,
When temptations me oppress,
And when I my sins confess,
Sweet Spirit, comfort me!

When I lie within my bed,
Sick in heart, and sick in head,
And with doubts discomfortèd,
Sweet Spirit, comfort me!

When the house doth sigh and weep,
And the world is drowned in sleep,
Yet mine eyes the watch do keep,
Sweet Spirit, comfort me! . . . .
When the artless doctor sees
No one hope, but of his fees,
And his skill runs on the lees,
Sweet Spirit, comfort me!

When his potion and his pill,
His, or none, or little skill,
Meet for nothing but to kill,
Sweet Spirit, comfort me! . . . .

When, God knows, I'm tossed about,
Either with despair or doubt;

Yet before the glass be out,
Sweet Spirit, comfort me!

Robert Herrick (1591-1674),
A Prayer to the Holy Spirit in a Time of Incurable
Illness.

Was Jesus ever reluctant to heal the sick? There were certainly occasions when he *"passed by"* sick people, without offering them any help. On other occasions he healed one or two people, but made no attempt to set anyone else free. Sometimes he passed people by, but then, when they pursued him, willingly gave them the miracle they craved. There is probably something to learn from all of those occasions, but here I want to focus upon two special accounts. They tell how Christ was apparently exasperated by someone's demand for a miracle. What shall we make of them? –

AN ENCOUNTER WITH A NOBLEMAN (JN 4:46-54)

Some teachers have claimed that Christ gave much time to healing the sick, not because he wanted to, but because he was driven to it by the people. They quote, for example, Jesus' remark to the nobleman: *"Unless you see signs and wonders, you will not believe"* (Jn 4:48).

In conjunction with that passage, at least one commentator has quoted *Mark 1:14-15* (which describes the same period in Jesus' ministry) to prove Jesus did not really want to spend so much time in healing; his main desire was to preach the gospel and to urge the people to repentance.

However, that writer, and others like him, forget that Matthew also records the same period, giving more detail than Mark, and he tells how Jesus not only preached the gospel but also –

> *cured every sickness and every illness among the people . . . so they brought to him everyone who was sick. Among them were people who were afflicted with various diseases and pains, demoniacs, epileptics, and paralytics, and he made them all well again (Mt 4:23-24).*

As a result, *"huge crowds followed him"* (vs. 25), to whom he preached *"the good news of the kingdom"*.

The picture conveyed by Matthew is hardly one of a reluctant Christ being forced to engage in a healing ministry! On the contrary, among other reasons, Jesus apparently healed the sick as a means of attracting people to listen to the preaching of the gospel. Healing the sick and preaching the gospel were inseparable components of the total ministry of Christ.

Well then, since the record plainly shows Jesus was not reluctant to heal, what meaning lies in his seemingly grudging words to the nobleman?

CHRIST WAS STATING A SIMPLE FACT

It is perfectly true that people do need to see evidence before they will believe. Every good preacher weaves into his sermons numerous testimonies of the transforming power of Christ. Doctrine must be substantiated by example, and affirmations by personal experience (cp. 1 Jn 1:1-4). And who can doubt that a great miracle of healing does provide powerful supportive proof of the gospel of Christ? Only a living, all-powerful Physician can heal continually, as he does! Furthermore, that God is willing to confirm his word and to encourage faith by *"signs, wonders, and miracles"* is shown in many places, in both *Old* and *New* *Testaments*.

CHRIST WANTED TO IDENTIFY THIS MAN

Note that in the original Greek text the pronoun *"you"* is plural – in other words it refers to a *group* of people not just to the *nobleman*. But which group? Some commentators suggest that the pronoun refers to people generally, and may have been a rebuke of the common curiosity about the supernatural. But it may also have been (as I have already suggested) a statement of simple fact – people often cannot be drawn to faith in God unless they see a demonstration of his power.

Other commentators think that Christ initially viewed the nobleman as a member of one of the two groups who had already scornfully demanded a *"sign"* from him – that is, either the Jews (cp. Jn 2:18), or Herod's officials (cp. Lu 23:8). Those groups wanted to see miracles merely for the sake of miracles, not out of any reverence for God, nor any interest in the gospel Christ was preaching. Christ may have identified the nobleman (presumably one of Herod's courtiers) with one or both of those groups. If so, he may have been hoping to see the Lord perform a prodigy like some kind of oriental magician. Jesus had to make sure the man's request was genuine, arising from real need and a true desire to encounter the power of God in Christ.

The nobleman's response showed the sincerity of his cry for help. He ignored the possible rebuke in Christ's remarks. He scarcely even heard what Jesus said. He simply repeated with greater passion and urgency his plea for Jesus to *"come down before my child dies"*. The Master was satisfied. Without further delay he spoke the word of authority and the nobleman knew his son was healed!

CHRIST WANTED TO DEAL WITH HIS SPIRITUAL NEED

Here is another suggestion: although the courtier came to Jesus on behalf of his son, and had faith in Christ as a healer sent by God, he had not yet seen that the first essential was to make matters right in his own soul. So the Lord endeavoured to lift the man's eyes away from the ministry of *signs* to the ministry of *salvation*.

The father had to see that his need for salvation was actually more imperative than his boy's need of healing. *"Unless"* is the key word here. *"Unless"* he had hoped to obtain a miracle he would not have come to Jesus at all. But the Lord knew his heart, struck home at the sole reason for his approach, and tried to direct the nobleman's attention to his personal need of spiritual healing. Jesus succeeded in that aim. The gospel happily reports, *"he himself believed, along with all his household"* (vs. 53).

CHRIST WAS SEEKING TO AROUSE GENUINE FAITH

The story as told in the gospel does imply that the courtier's approach to Christ was, at least in some measure, based upon belief in Jesus as a worker of magic, rather than confidence that he spoke with the authority of God. Hence the courtier urged Jesus to *"come down"* to his house, to demonstrate his power, and then perhaps the noble family would *"believe"*.

But the Lord threw at him the direct challenge to believe first, without seeing. The courtier failed to grasp Christ's meaning, and he kept on pleading, *"Sir, come down before my child dies!"* Then Christ spoke again. But this time his words were different. They were alive with power. They wrought an amazing transformation in the rich man. Jesus said: *"Go now, for your son will live!"*

And immediately the father believed!

He saw nothing. He felt nothing. But he knew his son was healed! Why? Because *"he believed the word that Jesus spoke to him"*. Christ spoke only five words. But those words possessed creative power. They banished the man's fear; they created faith; they revealed to him what Jesus really wanted from him – not to search for a miracle for its own sake, but to discover the God of all miracles through faith in the word of Christ.

That spiritual lesson is still relevant today: true faith has no need of special signs and wonders for its encouragement; it does not need the physical presence of Jesus. True faith is content to go its way, confident that what God has spoken will come to pass. Scripture expresses this same spiritual law elsewhere –

> *Whatever you ask in prayer, believe that you have received it, and you will (Mk 11:24) . . ...We have this confidence in Christ: we know that if we ask anything according to his will he hears us; and if we know that he hears us, then we know that we have already gained what we asked him to do (1 Jn 5:14-15).*

AN ENCOUNTER WITH THE PHARISEES

The Pharisees demanded a sign from Jesus, which he refused to give them (Mt 12:38-40; Mk 8:11-12; Lu 11:29-30). Does that mean Christ was reluctant to perform miracles? Not if you accept the following ideas–

1) The Pharisees asked for a sign only to *"test"* Jesus. They were endeavouring to embarrass him, or to cause him to betray himself. With good reason he was angry with them. But when ordinary people came to him in humility and trust, with no other motive except to have their need met, Christ willingly gave them their heart's desire. Without hesitation he healed all who were sick.

2) The Pharisees wanted a *"sign from heaven"* – that is, some spectacular miracle, such as calling down fire from heaven (as Elijah did), or making the sun stand still (as Joshua did), or turning the shadow

back ten degrees (as Isaiah did). This is the same temptation Satan pressed on Christ, *"Jump down from the pinnacle of the temple – amaze the multitudes by a stupendous miracle!"*

But Jesus scorned their provocation. To perform wonders of that sort would have been worthless display. He had come to heal those who were hurting, and for anyone whose heart was turned towards God, his miracles of healing were more than sufficient proof of his identity.

3)   But there is an obvious answer to any claim that Christ was reluctant to engage in a healing ministry. Just read the four gospels! How can anyone do so, and then say that Jesus healed the sick only under pressure and would have preferred to devote his time to teaching? Whatever Jesus meant by his words to the nobleman and to the Pharisees, he could not have meant that he was reluctant to spend time healing the sick. For despite what he said, he went right on curing thousands of people and working many *"signs, wonders, and miracles"* on behalf of those who believed in him.

Plainly, Jesus did not reckon that his reply to the malicious Pharisees, nor his gentle rebuke of the nobleman, placed any restriction on the miracles he wrought in answer to faith.

4)   If further proof is needed, turn to *Acts*. Plainly, the early church did not think their Lord was unwilling to work signs and wonders. On the contrary, they specifically prayed that he would (4:29-31); and then they went out themselves in his name to fulfil an amazing ministry of healing (5:12-16).

CHAPTER FOUR:

THE COVENANT IN ACTION

Speak low to me, my Saviour, low and sweet
From out the hallelujahs, sweet and low,
Lest I should fear and fall, and miss thee so
Who art not missed by any that entreat.
Speak to me as to Mary at thy feet!
And if no precious gums my hands bestow,
Let my tears drop like amber, while I go
In reach of thy divinest voice complete
In humanest affection – thus, in sooth,
To lose the sense of losing. As a child,
Whose song-bird seeks the wood for evermore,
Is sung to in its stead by mother's mouth
Till, sinking on her breast, love-reconciled,
He sleeps the faster that he wept before. [9]

This chapter looks at some dramatic aspects of how Christ fulfilled the healing covenant, and how people received healing at his hand – Scripture says –

> *For this purpose was the Son of God manifested, that he might destroy the works of the devil (1 Jn 3:8, KJV).*

Of course, he came not just to destroy the works of the devil during the three years of his public ministry but to maintain this warfare against Satan through every generation. Nonetheless, his purpose must apply

---

(9) Elizabeth Barrett Browning (1806-1861), <u>Comfort Me, Saviour</u>.

also to those three years. So our first question must be: "What is meant by 'the works of the devil'?" Many things could be named, but we are here concerned with one only, namely, *disease*. But some will say, "Is sickness really a work of the devil? Does Satan really cause illness?" The Bible's answer to that is an emphatic *"Yes!"* Proof is found in the following –

SATAN AND SICKNESS

1) There is an intimate connection between demon possession and sickness

- Mt 8:16,28-34; 9:32-33; 12:22-30; 15:22; 17:14-15; Mk 1:23-28; 5:1-20; Lu 4:33-37, 40-41; 8:2,26-36; 9:1-2,37-42; 19:9,17; 11:14; 13:10-17.

- in all those instances, healing came as soon as the demons were driven out of the people, thus showing clearly that their ailments were caused by satanic power.

2) Jesus specifically stated that certain people were bound by the devil – for example, Lu 13:16.

3) Jesus stated that

- sickness was part of Satan's kingdom
- only someone who was stronger than Satan could heal the sick and cast out demons
- the purpose of the kingdom of God was to deliver those who were bound, and that
- his healing ministry was clear evidence the kingdom of God had come (Mt 12:22-29).

Notice the biting sarcasm in the challenge Jesus gave to the Pharisees, *"By whom do your followers cast them out?"* He knew, and they knew, that neither they nor their followers had any power to cast out demons. Yet it was obvious to the Lord, and should have been to the Pharisees, that healing the sick delivered a shattering blow to the kingdom of darkness. This ministry of deliverance was therefore one in which all true servants of God should be active (vs. 25-27).

They had accused Jesus of working in league with the devil. But, in the light of their own failure to heal the sick and cast out demons, the Lord scornfully showed how their attempt to discredit him was merely pitiful.

Further, he conclusively proved that his opposition to the kingdom of darkness, as demonstrated by removing sickness and oppression, was evidence of his divine mission and power (vs. 28-29).

Then he insisted that all who were, like he, opposed to the devil, should also join with him in driving out the devil's oppressions, and in gathering men and women into the kingdom of God (vs. 30).

The kingdom of God has indeed come unto us when the sick are healed and demons are driven out by the name of Jesus (vs. 28).

The Lord gave a commission to his disciples to go and *"heal the sick and cast out demons"*. No limitation was placed on that command. They were told plainly to heal the sick – all the sick, any sick, especially those who believed the gospel and had faith in the healing power of God.

That all-inclusive commission is itself proof that

- it is God's will to heal all who are sick
- sickness does not come from God
- sickness is ultimately the work of the devil, and that
- all true servants of God will obey the Lord's command to bring healing to those who are ill and oppressed, in Jesus' name.

See Mt 10:1,7-8; Mk 16:15-18; Lu 9:1-2; 10:1,9; and the following –

HEALING THE OPPRESSED

Peter once summarised the ministry of Christ in these dramatic words –

> *God anointed Jesus of Nazareth with the Holy Spirit and with power, so that everywhere he went he worked good things and healed everyone who was oppressed by the devil; for God was with him (Ac 10:38).*

At once we learn four strong things about Christ –

1) Jesus of Nazareth was *"anointed by God"* – that is, he was filled with the Holy Spirit and with power. His ministry of teaching and of

healing were both wrought in the strength of that divine anointing. Thus he set an example for all who follow him.

2) This anointing was given for the express purpose of enabling Christ to go about among the people and to do good things, which meant bringing them the blessing of God, and showing them the way to a more abundant life.

3) Whatever the Master did was good: he was good himself; he did good; he brought good to men and women. Did he preach the gospel? Then preaching is a good work. Did he heal the sick? Then healing the sick is a good work. Did he cast out demons? Then casting out demons is a good work. We his servants should be content to be as he was and to do as he did. He went around doing good and healing the sick. His church should do the same.

He healed the sick because it was a good work. If healing the sick is a good work, then sickness must be a bad work. If healing the sick is a good work, which comes from the anointing of God, then sickness must be a bad work that comes from the devil!

4) He healed *all* who were oppressed by the devil. That statement can be taken two ways –

- it may mean that every person who is sick is oppressed by Satan, so that all disease has a satanic origin

- or it may mean only that the people Jesus healed were oppressed by Satan – in other words, he did not heal anyone unless it was evident to him that the devil was the author of their suffering.

There is little practical difference between the two statements.

The first one, that all who are sick are oppressed by the devil, would have to be qualified in the ways that have already been indicated in the first part of this study, [10] and also elsewhere in this book. But the second of them, that Jesus healed only those whose sickness stemmed from Satan, would have to be qualified by remembering the vast number of people healed by Jesus – it could not be used to prove that only a few

---

(10) I mean, the associated book, Healing in the Whole Bible – Old Testament. See, in particular, the section that deals with the biblical *Book of Job*.

people are afflicted by Satan. On the contrary, the evidence offered by the ministry of Jesus is that sickness should almost always be considered an enemy, one to be opposed by every means at our disposal.

I know that the question of sickness as a discipline inflicted by God cannot be ignored, and it will be discussed again in later chapters. But here I am content to press home the message that is overwhelmingly presented in scripture: sickness is an oppression of Satan, and those who, like their Master, desire to go about doing good by the Holy Spirit, will set themselves to oppose it in the name of Jesus.

SETTING THE CAPTIVES FREE

See *Luke 4:18-19*. The various parts of that prophecy may be given a spiritual rather than a physical significance. Yet it is also plain from the things Jesus did in the anointing of the Holy Spirit, that he considered sickness to be a captivity, a bruising, darkening influence antagonistic to the Spirit of God. The *"acceptable year of the Lord"* has not yet passed away. This is still the day of God's grace. If the work of the Holy Spirit in the dawning hour of this day of mercy was to loose those who were bruised in the captivity of sickness, it must still be his work, for the night-time of judgment has not yet come. And if sickness is bondage, it must be a captivity brought on by Satan, for the Spirit of God does not war against the work of God.

See *John 10:10*. Whatever steals, whatever kills, whatever destroys, is the handiwork of the enemy of our souls. He is described as *"prowling around like a roaring lion, seeking someone to devour"* (1 Pe 5:8). And what steals away the happiness of men and women, what robs their strength and security, what kills their ambitions and breaks their dreams, what devours their hopes and wrecks their lives, more than sickness?

The Master used plain words in his teaching, and he surely intended them to have their ordinary meaning. So I assume that he meant just what he said when he proclaimed, *"I have come that you might discover life, and enjoy it more abundantly!"* Life and disease are opposite concepts. In disease there is no life – only pain, misery, and eventually death. But Jesus came to give us life and to give it ***abundantly***!

Surely that is the basic desire of God for all who receive Christ as Saviour? And surely, proffering a life free from crippling pain and destructive disease will ordinarily fulfill that divine promise? Such works of death come from Satan. But from the hand of God we normally have a right to expect those things that comprise a rich, happy, and healthy life.

Notice the adverbs "ordinarily" and "normally". Those qualifiers are necessary, because scripture does show that sometimes the promise of abundant life may be fulfilled in a form other than good health and material prosperity.

For example: during times of persecution it may take the form of divinely-given courage, and of joy in the midst of suffering. Or, in times of political and national upheaval, it may take the form of the providence of God preserving his people from fear, ruin, starvation, and from the worst effects of the upheaval. Or, some higher purpose of God for his children may cause him to deal with them as he did with Job.

But such cases are extraordinary. They are exceptions to the rule. The overwhelming witness of scripture is that we should give an ordinary meaning to the words *"abundant life"*. The promise may occasionally have a more subtle outworking, but for most of us most of the time it entitles us to claim from God a life free of disease and enriched by his favour and blessing. That is what we should continue to expect from God, unless larger circumstances, or some personal word from heaven, make it plain that your life, or mine, must take a different course.

WHOSE SIDE ARE YOU ON?

Scripture states that Christ came to destroy the works of the devil. Therefore, whatever Jesus opposed and destroyed during his public ministry must be viewed as a work of the devil. Did he fight sickness? Did he seek to destroy disease whenever he faced it? Did he strive to cure illness wherever he found it?

There is only one possible answer!

Basically, then, sickness must be reckoned a work of Satan. That is why Christ went around healing all who were sick – he did not find one person of whom it could be properly said their affliction was the will of God. Disease is a product of the kingdom of darkness; but God has brought us into the kingdom of his dear Son (Cl 1:13). Therefore we are now entitled to rise up in faith, to resist the devil, knowing he will flee from us (Ja. 4:7), and confidently to claim healing from the Lord.

CHAPTER FIVE:

HOW PEOPLE RECEIVED HEALING

. . . .

Is the truce broke? or 'cause we have
A Mediator now with thee,
Dost thou therefore old treaties waive
And by appeals from them decree?

Or is't so, as some green heads say,
That now all miracles must cease?
Though thou hast promised they should stay
The tokens of the Church, and peace.

No, no; religion is a spring
That from some secret, golden mine
Derives her birth, and thence doth bring
Cordials in every drop, and wine;

But in her long and hidden course
Passing through the earth's dark veins,
Grows still from better unto worse,
And both her taste and colour stains. . . . .

Heal these waters, Lord; or bring thy flock,
Since these are troubled, to the springing Rock;
Look down, great Master of the Feast; O shine,
And turn once more our water into wine!

— Henry Vaughan (1622-1695), A Prayer.

The four gospels reveal a number of bases upon which people were able to receive healing from Christ. A study of those foundations shows that they are as applicable today as they were in Bible days.

A SOVEREIGN ACT OF GOD

Healing does not always result from a personal appropriation of the covenant; it may also stem from a simple act of divine sovereignty. In such cases the personal faith of the sick person may be of minimal importance. There are two major categories into which healing as an act of divine sovereignty may fall –

A TIME OF VISITATION

In *Luke 19:44* Jesus speaks about the people not knowing *"the time of their visitation"*. That unusual phrase relates to the three years of Jesus' public ministry, during which there was an amazing display of divine healing. Multitudes thronged Christ and were healed either by his touch upon them (Lu 4:40) or by their touch upon him (Mt 14:36). It cannot be imagined that all of those people possessed strong faith. Many of them must have had little or no awareness of who Jesus really was. Some thought he was a re-incarnated prophet, others that he was a new prophet raised up by God. A few recognised him as the Messiah, while still others may have seen him only as a specially powerful sorcerer (cp. Mt 16:13-16).

Some people did have pure and vigorous faith in Christ. But there were many others who observed only that Jesus of Nazareth displayed an incredible ability to heal the sick, and they hastened to take advantage of it while they could. Christ (as we shall discuss in a moment) did endeavour to arouse in the people a more genuine expression of faith; but he nonetheless gave healing even to those whose faith was minimal. It was a time of visitation, and the power and glory of God were richly displayed in order to draw the nation to repentance. The people failed, however, to recognise what was happening and suffered the dreadful consequences (Lu 19:41-44).

So then, while the healing covenant usually demands an exercise of true belief *in* and appropriation *of* the promise of God, there are times of divine visitation when the extraordinary replaces the ordinary. Those times may come to a church, a town, a nation, a generation, and during them the magnanimity of God spills far beyond the covenant, embracing all who respond even slightly.

CONFIRMATION OF THE WORD

Several places in the NT speak of God using *"signs, wonders, and miracles"* to confirm the truth of his word (cp. Mk 16:20; Ac 2:22; Ro 15:19; 1 Th 1:5; He 2:4). The situation in those cases is the same as the one we have just discussed: even when faith is virtually non-existent, the Lord may choose to confirm his word to some people by granting them a miracle. He is sovereign in heaven and may do as he pleases on earth (except that he cannot act against his own integrity, Ps 135:6; Ja 1:17)).

That does not remove from us the need to develop proper faith and to approach God within the framework of the covenant. But it does mean that God is free, if he so chooses, to extend his mercy beyond the covenant, and thus seek to draw people to align themselves with the covenant. If they reject his mercy and refuse to believe his word, then no recourse is left to heaven except to apply the penal clauses of the covenant.

A PROPERLY STRUCTURED FAITH

Generally speaking, before people could receive healing from Christ he expected them to approach him in a certain way. Jesus was not haphazard in his ministry to the sick – he continually endeavoured to elicit from them a definite response of faith. Not all came to him in the same way, not all had the same faith, not all observed all the things I am going to mention. Nonetheless, Jesus did try to establish the principle that people should do whatever is required to complete their faith and to bring them into contact with the healing power of God. The same rule applies today.

Here then are some of the things that comprise a properly structured faith.

KNOW THAT CHRIST IS WILLING TO HEAL

"Lord, if you choose, you can make me whole," pleaded the leper. He knew that the *ability* of Christ was equal to his *need*, but he was unsure that Jesus *wanted* to cure him. The Lord's immediate response was a kindly and confident, *"I will: be clean!"* And at once the man was made completely whole.

That miracle of healing is the first one specifically detailed in the gospel (Mt 8:1-3). What moved the Holy Spirit to place this incident at the beginning of the inspired record of Jesus' healing ministry? Probably to make it plain that Christ is willing, always, to heal those who come to him in proper faith.

From that time on the Lord continued to give positive evidence of his willingness to heal everyone by the simple fact that he actually *did* cure *all* who came to him for healing! (see Mt 4:24; 8:16; 14:14; etc.)

KNOW THAT CHRIST IS ABLE TO HEAL

"Do you believe that I can do this?" Christ demanded of the two blind men. Their prompt response was a bold, *"Yes, Lord!"* Then Christ touched their eyes, saying, *"According to your faith, so let it be done for you!"* And at once their eyes were opened (Mt 9:27-31).

When people came to him, the Lord knew at once where their faith needed strengthening. To one he said, *"Fear not;"* to another, *"I will;"* to another, *"All things are possible with God;"* to another, *"All things are possible for you, if you believe."*

Some he took aside and ministered to privately; on some he laid his hands; others he permitted to touch him. Some he commanded to act on their own faith, saying, *"Stand up, pick up your bed, and walk,"* or *"Stretch out your hand."* Others he anointed with oil; to some he only spoke a word of commanding faith; for others he offered prayer. Each person was different, and to each one the Lord ministered in whatever way would best encourage their faith and help them to make contact with his healing power.

In the case of the two blind men who cried out, *"Son of David, have mercy on us,"* the Lord sensed a desperation that was not truly faith. So he stilled them, and then bluntly challenged them to confess faith in his power to meet their need. His confidence inspired them; his word generated a greater assurance within them; and their positive response (*"Yes, Lord!"*) at once made it possible for Christ to give them the miracle they desired. Immediately after, Jesus gave a graphic demonstration of his ability to heal all who trust him, no matter what their affliction may be, by going out and *"curing* **every** *sickness and* **every** *disease among the people"* (vs. 35; 4:23).

RECEIVE THE GOSPEL

Wherever Christ went, before he began healing the sick he preached the gospel (Mt 4:23; 9:35; Mk 1:14-15; Lu 4:18; Mt 11:5; Lu 7:22). Only those therefore who were willing to listen to the gospel were able to go further and trust him for healing. Rejection of the message he preached (as shown, for example, by the scribes and Pharisees) inevitably destroyed faith in his power to heal, or else led to a denunciation of his healing ministry (Mt 9:34; etc).

OVERCOME FEAR

It is not possible to maintain faith, and at the same time be dominated by fear – that is, by doubt, worry, anxiety, or despair. So, no matter how desperate the situation, the Lord insisted that people should master their emotions, be rid of fear, and *believe only* (Mk 5:21-24,35-36; Lu 8:41-42,49-50).

ACKNOWLEDGE THE AUTHORITY OF HIS WORD

Christ was deeply pleased and moved by those who realised the authority of his spoken word, and who needed no more than this to bring them deliverance. Thus a Roman centurion displayed the greatest faith ever witnessed by Christ; a faith based simply on knowing that the healing power of God did not lie in the personal presence of Jesus but in his word. The centurion did not actually meet the Master, nor did he want him to come to his house. The soldier merely said, *"Just speak the word, and my servant will be made well!"* (Lu 7:1-10).

We are in the same position: we cannot see Jesus, neither can he come physically to our side; but we do have his word, and much more of that word than was given to the centurion! Unwavering faith in the authority and power of the word of Christ will bring the same result for us as it did for the soldier.

Another example is seen in the faith of the nobleman who came to ask Jesus to heal his son. The Lord merely said to him, *"Go home, for your boy will live!"* The father's reaction was quite remarkable, and must have pleased the Lord greatly: *"the man believed what Jesus had told him, and he at once turned back home"* (Jn 4:50).

But the most striking thing about that story is the contrast between the father's former desperation and his final quiet assurance. The change was almost instantaneous. One moment, in terror lest his son should die, he was urgently begging Jesus to hurry down to his house. The next moment, under the impact of the word of Christ, his fear and desperation had vanished, and calm faith had taken their place.

The distance between Cana and Capernaum (vs. 46), was no more than 40 kilometres, and Jesus spoke to the man about one o'clock in the afternoon. Being a nobleman he could probably have travelled home that same day. He certainly began his journey straight away, yet delayed his actual return until the next day (vs. 52). Surely this overnight stay shows how completely he trusted the promise of Christ – he knew that his son was already swiftly recovering.

This change in the man, the healing of the boy, and the salvation of his entire household (vs. 53), were all wrought simply through unwavering trust in the word Jesus had spoken.

TURN FROM SIN

One of the primary aims of Jesus' healing ministry was to enable people to live righteously and to devote their health and strength to the glory of God.

Consequently he warned them often against using their new-found health for evil purposes. *"Stop committing sin,"* he cautioned, *"otherwise something worse may befall you!"* (Jn 5:14).

FERVENT PRAYER

The exciting account of the two blind men who cried out to Jesus for mercy, and who would not be silenced, is a vivid example of the impact that fervent prayer makes on the Lord (Mt 20:29-34). Insistently, passionately, they shouted above the noise of the crowd. Their faith was not one of calm assurance (such as the Roman centurion), it was a faith impelled by the strength of their need and the urgency of reaching Christ before he passed beyond their reach.

Jesus stopped and called out, *"What do you want?"* Scarcely able to believe their ears they flung their impassioned plea at him, *"Lord! give us back our sight!"* Moved with compassion, the Lord went over, touched their eyes, and immediately they were cured. Fervent prayer, prayer that refuses to be denied, prayer that takes advantage of the opportunity of the hour, still moves Christ to sympathy and an act of power (see Mt 11:12; Lu 11:9; Ja 5:17; also cp. Mk 7:32; Lu 4:38; 9:38; etc.)

SET A TIME AND A PLACE

The woman who had suffered from a haemorrhage for twelve years *"said to herself, 'If I can just touch his robe, I shall be made well.'"* (Mt 9:21). Many others heard about this miracle. So when Christ returned some time later to the same place, *"the people who lived there recognised him. So they sent word around the whole region and brought to him everyone who was sick. They begged him to let them touch even the fringe of his garment; and everyone who did so was made well!"* (Mt 14:34-36).

Those people all set a *place* and a *time* (the moment they touched his robe) to release their faith. At that instant, they believed that his healing power would pour into them; and indeed, in response to their faith, virtue did flow out of him and they were made whole. And there are other examples –

- some people found in the touch of his hand the time of their contact with the power of Christ (Mk 8:23-25; Lu 4:49; 13:13)

- others found it when they were anointed with oil (Mk 6:13)

- some, like the Roman centurion, required the Lord merely to *"speak the word"*

- one man's contact of faith came when he had washed in the pool (Jn 9:7-11)

- another, when Christ came into his house and laid hands on his sick daughter (Mt 9:18).

In each case there was a specific moment when the people believed with all their heart that the power of God was linked with their need. At that moment they knew that their prayer was answered and the work was done.

We, too, should make use of a point of contact.

BOLDLY ACT

A demand for action was a common part of the Lord's approach to the healing ministry –

- he urged a blind man to start looking (Mk 8:23)

- he told another to stretch out his withered hand (Mk 3:1-5)

- another had to *"pick up his bed and walk"* (Mt 9:6; Jn 5:8)

- another was commanded to *"go on your way"*, believing that healing was wrought (Jn 4:50; Lu 17:14)

- another had to roll the stone away from the tomb (Jn 11:39-40)

- still another had to go and wash in the pool (Jn 9:7-11).

In all those instances the Lord required people to demonstrate their faith by some definite action. Those who could not see were to start looking, those whose limbs were crippled or deformed were to stretch them out, and so on.

Such actions of faith brought their believing power into full release, and turned loose the life of God into their afflicted bodies. The words of James are significant in this connection – *"Faith without works (or corresponding action) is dead!"* (Ja 2:17).

EXPRESS GRATITUDE

One of the most poignant sayings of Jesus was addressed to a leper: *"Where are the other nine?"* Ten lepers had been cured by Christ, but only one returned to give glory to God, and he was a Samaritan (Lu 17:11-14). Of the nine it is said only that they were *"cured"*. But to this man Jesus said, *"Your faith has made you whole"* (the Greek word is *sozo*, and it means "saved/healed/restored" in the fullest sense).

Some commentators reckon that the use of *sozo* here implies that the other nine lepers, although they were cured of leprosy, still bore on their bodies the scars and deformities inflicted by the disease. But the Samaritan was fully restored; that is, his limbs were made perfectly normal. No sign remained that he had ever had leprosy. Whether or not that was so, the passage still suggests that a deeper degree of healing (spiritually and physically) was gained by the Samaritan, because he returned to give thanks.

FAITH IS ESSENTIAL

It is true that many people who had little or no faith were healed by Christ, either as an expression of divine sovereignty or as an act of compassion (for example, it appears that the widow of Nain, and Malchus, did not display much faith – Lu 7:11-16; 22:51). Nonetheless,

Jesus normally did search for faith in those who came to him. In fact, in the face of definite unbelief he became almost powerless.

At Nazareth, for example, because of their unbelief, *"he could do no mighty work"* (Mk 6:1-6). Notice, it does not say he *would* not, but he *could* not. Their unbelief did not make him any less willing to heal, it just prevented him from extending his hand to meet their need. A few sick folks broke through the barrier and sought the Lord in faith; but the majority were left as they were. Christ went away distressed and amazed by their unbelief. The impression is strong that he must feel the same way about most of our communities today.

On another occasion, when the disciples were unable to cure an epileptic boy, Jesus complained, *"What faithless and perverse people you are! How long must I remain with you? How long do I have to bear with you?"* Bluntly the Lord told the disciples that unbelief was the sole cause of their failure; and then he went on to remind them of the tremendous power of faith (vs .20). True faith in God, he said, would enable them to speak with such authority that they could move a mountain – *"nothing will be impossible for you."*

We are accustomed to thinking that all things are possible for *God*, but Christ showed that all things are also possible for *us*! To the father of the boy the Lord said much the same (Mk 9:23). The man had challenged Jesus, *"If you can do anything, help us!"* But Christ retorted, *"If you can believe, all things are possible for someone who believes!"*

The need was faith.

And so it is today. There is no doubt about the ability of God to do anything that does not deny his own character. But he is sparing of the supernatural. Usually, before he decides to do some "impossible" thing, he looks for faith. But if we show the same kind of faith that people did in the gospel stories, then we may expect Christ to do for us the same mighty works he did for them.

Time and again the Lord intimated to people that their own faith was responsible for the healing they had gained. To quote only one of many examples, Christ said to blind Bartimaeus, *"Go on your way, your faith has made you whole"* (Mk 10:46-52). There Jesus placed greater emphasis upon personal faith than upon his own power. By so doing he showed the vast potential of faith.

Further indication of the necessity for faith, and of the certainty that true faith will attract the healing virtue of the Lord (Lu 6:19; 8:46) is found in the number of times the idea of faith is connected with the healing ministry of Christ –

- *"faith"*, Mt 8:10; 9:2,22,29; 15:28; 17:20; Mk 2:5; 5:34; 10:52; Lu 5:20; 7:9,50; 8:48; 17:19; 18:42.

- *"faithless"*, Mt 17:17; Mk 9:19; Lu 9:41.

- *"believe"*, Mt 9:28; Mk 5:36; 9:23-24; 16:17; Lu 8:50; Jn 4:38; 9:35-36,38; 11:40.

- *"believed"*, Mt 8:13; Jn 4:50.

- *"unbelief"*, Mt 13:48; 17:20; Mk 6:6; 9:24.

Closely associated with those examples are the incidents when Christ hushed the storm and cursed the fig tree (Mt 8:26; 14:31; 21:21-22; Mk 4:40; 11:22-24; Lu 8:25).

In each of those references the Lord placed tremendous emphasis upon the importance of faith.

But the four most pungent sayings are these, and warrant writing again:

> *"If you believe, all things are possible to anyone who believes."*

> *"Whatever you ask in prayer, believing, you shall receive."*

> *"As you have believed, so it will be done for you."*

> *"According to your faith, so it will be done for you."*

Those statements, all spoken by Jesus, plainly declare that the measure of our receiving *from* God is the measure of our believing *in* God!

CHAPTER SIX:

THE EIGHT SIGNS

Glorious the sun in mid career;
Glorious the assembled fires appear;
   Glorious the comet's train:
Glorious the trumpet and alarm;
Glorious the almighty stretched-out arm;
   Glorious the enraptured main: . . . .

Glorious – more glorious is the crown
Of him that brought salvation down,
   By meekness called thy Son; [11]
Thou that stupendous truth believed, [12]
And now the matchless deed's achieved,
   Determined, dared, and done! [13]

"Now Jesus did many other signs in the presence of the disciples, which are not written in this book; but these are written that you may believe that Jesus is the Christ,

---

(11) The line is addressed to King David, and the reference here is to the humble willingness of Christ to be known as David's descendent. The poem was composed either during or just after Mr Smart's confinement for four years in a private hospital for mentally disturbed people. It is "a celebration of Creation and the Incarnation, (and is) built on a mathematical and mystical ordering of stanzas grouped in threes, fives, and sevens, and was compared by Robert Browning . . . to a great cathedral in its structure and imagery." (The Oxford Companion to English Literature)

(12) That is, David believed in the promise of the coming Messiah, which has now been stunningly fulfilled in and by Christ.

(13) From A Song to David, by Christopher Smart (1722-1771).

the Son of God, and that believing you may have life in his name" (Jn 20:30-31).

I n those words John highlights the focus of his gospel: here is the conclusion toward which he steadfastly intended to lead us. Three key words stand out: *signs*; *believe*; *life*.

SIGNS

The miracles of Jesus are called signs because they were wrought for a purpose. They were a witness of what he had come to do, an indication of the will of God for his people, a confirmation of the nature of the gospel, a demonstration of the proper direction for life.

John carefully selected eight of these signs, and built his gospel around them. Apart from the resurrection of Christ, these eight miracles are the only ones recorded by John. The apostle himself called them signs (2:11,23; 3:2; 4:54; 6:2; 20:30), and he declared that out of the *"many other signs"* Jesus did, he had selected these *eight* to exemplify the nature of Christ and to draw his readers to faith.

Here then are eight miracles

- that reveal the wonder of Christ, the Son of God
- that show the things he desires us to receive
- that teach us what direction our faith should take, and
- that reveal the marvellous life we can discover in his name!

The eight signs are –

1. turning water into wine (2:1-11)

2. healing the court official's son (4:46-54)

3. healing the cripple at Bethesda (5:1-17)

4. feeding five thousand people (6:1-13)

5. hushing the storm (6:16-21)

6. healing the blind man (9:1-41)

7. raising Lazarus from death (11:1-46)

8. the incredible catch of fish (21:3-8)

Notice that four of those signs (that is, half of them) were miracles of *healing*.

BELIEVE

The signs were not miracles wrought only for their own sake. The mighty works of Christ were performed and recorded for a major purpose: *to draw from us a faith response*.

In particular, they provide compelling proof of the divinity of Christ, so that we, confronted by these superb deeds, are constrained to emulate Thomas and cry out, *"My Lord and my God!"* (Jn 20:28). We cannot doubt that these things happened, because they are all subsumed in the greatest miracle of all, the resurrection of Jesus from the dead.

LIFE

The signs draw us to believe, and the result of this belief is *"life in his name"*. But what form does that life take? How is it to be expressed? What are its component parts? What things can we expect Christ to do for us?

The eight signs encourage us to believe that Christ seeks to bring us from–

FORMALISM TO FAITH

SIGN ONE: THE WATER THAT BECAME WINE

The stone jars into which the servants poured water and from which they drew wine, were normally used *"for the Jewish rites of purification"* (2:6). John took special notice of that fact, which seems to indicate that he saw in this miracle more than just a wonderful work. There was here a special sign. It symbolised the cold emptiness of the old religion contrasted with the zestful dynamic of the gospel of Christ. It indicated that Christ is ever willing to take hold of the stony formality of religious tradition, to touch it (and its practitioners) with a miracle, and to transform it into the new wine of abundant life.

The operative word is *abundant*. For you will notice that the six jars each held *"approximately 100 litres."* That is a lot of wine!

DISEASE TO HEALTH

SIGN TWO: A DYING BOY MADE WELL

As I have shown above, the healing of the court official's son was only one of many miracles Jesus wrought during a short period of phenomenal display of healing power. Hundreds of people were cured at that time, of almost every conceivable infirmity. The crowds flocked to Christ; and while his main desire was to teach them, and to draw from them a higher expression of faith and a deeper commitment to God (as shown by his conversation with the nobleman), still he turned no-one away. He healed everyone who came to him, thus plainly demonstrating his deep opposition to disease, and his yearning to release people from their afflictions.

This sign identifies Jesus as the *Great Physician*; it points us to the healing covenant; it encourages us today to emulate the nobleman boldly by pleading with Christ to come as he did of old, and to heal us too!

HELPLESSNESS TO STRENGTH

SIGN THREE: A CRIPPLE WALKS AGAIN

The healing of the cripple at Bethesda was a great miracle, yet the most moving part of the story is the paralysed man's complaint that no one would help him. But then Christ helped him, by making him whole so that he could help himself!

The particular Christian experience this sign foreshadowed was described by Paul in these words –

> *I keep on asking the Father to help you grasp the limitless measure of his power, which is at work in everyone who believes. That power acts in us just as it did in Christ when by his mighty strength God raised him from the dead and then enthroned him at his right hand in the heavenlies. . . . I pray also, in proportion to his glorious riches, that he may cause you to be inwardly and powerfully strengthened through his Spirit. (Ep 1:15-23; 3:14-21).*

HUNGER TO SATISFACTION

SIGN FOUR: FEEDING AN IMMENSE CROWD

Several of these eight signs reflect the *eight covenant names* of God that are discussed in *Healing in the Whole Bible – Old Testament –*

- those signs that embody a healing miracle reveal Christ as *Yahweh-Rapha*, the Great Physician

- the miracle of hushing the storm shows Christ as *Yahweh-Shalom*, the Prince of Peace

- when he called Lazarus from the grave (a miracle that followed his own description of himself as *"the good shepherd"*, Jn 10:11) Jesus identified himself with *Yahweh-Raah*, the Shepherd who leads his sheep safely through the valley of the shadow of death

- that same miracle, set against the background of Jesus' words that he *"goes before"* his sheep and they *"follow him"* (Jn 10:3-4), reminds us of *Yahweh-Nissi* (*"The Lord our Banner"*) and of *Yahweh-Shammah* (*"The Lord Ever Present"*)

- and the sign we are now considering, the fourth, the miracle of feeding 5000 people with only five barley loaves and two fish, plainly portrays Christ as *Yahweh-Jireh* (*"The Lord our Provider"*)

- the two remaining titles, *Yahweh-Tsidkenu* (*"The Lord our Righteousness"*) and *Yahweh-Qadesh* (*"The Lord our Sanctifier"*), are probably implicit in each of the eight signs, and indeed in all that Jesus said and did.

AGITATION TO CALM

SIGN FIVE: THE HOWLING WIND STILLED

To hush a raging storm by the sheer power of his presence, and to transport a boat instantly to shore, reveals a spiritual authority, a command over circumstances, that is beyond measure. It is Christ's guarantee to us that no fear is so great he cannot quell it, no threat so perilous he cannot cause us to surmount it, no journey so hazardous (if he wills we should make it safely) that he cannot bring us to our goal.

To keep close to Christ is to keep within the calm eye of every hurricane that may surge across our lives.

DARKNESS TO LIGHT

SIGN SIX: A BLIND MAN SEES

The miracle of giving sight to a man who was born blind encourages faith in Christ as the Great Physician of both *body* and *soul*. As the poet said, "The eyes are the windows of the soul." That is, when Christ healed physical blindness he demonstrated also his power to heal spiritual blindness.

Paul understood that when he repeated the commission Christ had given him: *"Open the eyes of the Gentiles, so that they may turn from darkness to light and from the power of Satan to God."* Later, he rejoiced that *"God has delivered us from the dominion of darkness and transferred us to the kingdom of his beloved Son"* (Ac 26:18; Cl 1:13).

Peter also bade the people to *"declare the amazing works of God, who called you out of darkness and into his marvellous light"* (1 Pe 2:9).

DEATH TO LIFE

SIGN SEVEN: A DEAD MAN BROUGHT TO LIFE

Dare we see the raising of Lazarus as a valid paradigm for our time? Is such a miracle beyond the bounds of possibility today? Only to those who either deny the truth of scripture or limit the potential of faith in God!

Christ plainly instructed his disciples to follow his example, not only by healing the sick in his name, but also by raising the dead: *Matthew 10:8;* and cp. *Acts 9:36-43; 20:9-10*. Likewise, a comparison of *Matthew 10:8* with *4:23; 9:35* shows clearly that Christ commanded his disciples to continue doing all that they had seen him do. They were to proclaim the same gospel of the kingdom. They were to display the same miracles. The word was to be confirmed by the same signs and wonders. His ministry was to be expanded and continued through them.

Did he raise the dead? Then they were to do the same. And the same commission is given to the church today.

That does not mean, of course, that we can indiscriminately set ourselves against death. Neither Christ nor the disciples, nor the early church, were profligate in raising the dead. Death then was normally as final as it is now. It would be fair to infer that no dead person can be restored to life except by a special revelation of God's will and by a special impartation of faith. There is no valid theological reason why this should not still happen, and indeed, *it does!*

However, there is a deeper significance to the miracle of raising Lazarus from the dead: it demonstrates Christ's ability both to release us from the death of sin and, on the last day, to raise us up into eternal life. As surely as Lazarus was loosed from the grave clothes that bound him, so Christ can free us from the bondage of sin and bring us into his own glorious liberty. As surely as his voice called Lazarus out of the tomb, so will he call us from our graves to receive our heavenly inheritance (Jn 5:25-29).

FAILURE TO SUCCESS

SIGN EIGHT: AN AMAZING HAUL OF FISH

Many ingenious and often absurd attempts have been made to find some spiritual significance in the fact that just *153* large fish were caught (Jn 21:11). But it seems more natural to see the number as showing nothing more than the extraordinary nature of the catch. The disciples were so impressed by the miracle, they remembered the exact number of fish that had been caught.

It is no doubt possible to make various spiritual applications of the incident as a whole, and to draw various lessons from it; but the idea that lies most plainly on the surface is simply this: *Christ is willing to turn failure into success.*

As the disciples embarked on their mission to be *"fishers of men"* they were to do so not alone, but with Christ, and with confidence that he would give them great success.

But the promise is applicable not only to preachers. Whatever task life and the will of God may lay upon you, it is proper for you to consciously unite yourself with Christ and to expect that he will prosper you. That

John himself accepted this is shown by the words quoted elsewhere in these two volumes –

> *Beloved, I pray that you will prosper in every way, and*
> *that you will enjoy good health. (3 Jn 2)*

What then does God want us to have? Not mere existence, but *life*. Abundant life now (Jn 10:10). Eternal life hereafter (3:16). And this real, overflowing life is proffered to all who call upon God in the name of Christ. That these things are so is attested by the eight signs (19:35; 21:24), and their significance is plain: Jesus is proven to be the Christ, the Son of God, who has come to fulfil for us all the covenant promises of God.

CHAPTER SEVEN:

THE GOSPEL AND THE CROSS

> O holy Jesus who didst for us die,
>   And on the altar bleeding lie,
> Bearing all torment, pain, reproach and shame,
>   That we by virtue of the same,
> Though enemies to God, might be
> Redeemed and set at liberty.
> As thou didst us forgive,
> So meekly let us love to others show,
> And live in heaven on earth below. [14]

The Lord Jesus Christ embarked on his public ministry at the time of his baptism by John in the river Jordan. As he stood braced against the running waters, his hands and face lifted heavenward in prayer, the Holy Spirit descended upon him, and the voice of God spoke from heaven, *"You are my beloved Son; with you I am well pleased."* (Lu 3:21-22).

Shortly after this Christ began to preach everywhere in the power of the Spirit and his fame spread through the whole region (4:14-15).

Within a few weeks he came to Nazareth, where he had been brought up. As he had done many times before, on the Sabbath day he stood up in the synagogue to read the scripture (vs. 16). Now this was his first address in his home town as the anointed Messiah of Israel; it was given at the very beginning of his public ministry; it was given especial emphasis by Luke (4:18-19). It seems reasonable to accept this address as laying down the basic policy and purpose of Christ.

---

(14) Thomas Traherne (1637?-1674), <u>O Holy Jesus</u>.

Jesus claimed that he was the Messiah (Christ), the anointed one of God, the one sent by God to redeem Israel. He declared that God had placed upon him the Holy Spirit, and that this divine fulness had been given him for one basic purpose: *that he might preach –*

THE PREACHING SAVIOUR

Christ clearly stated the three-fold nature of the message he was called and anointed to preach –

ANOINTED TO PREACH GOOD NEWS

Two powerful themes were continually threaded through the preaching of Jesus of Nazareth –

THE PROCLAMATION OF MERCY

Jesus constantly sounded the good news of God's mercy to those who were bankrupt in their souls because of sin; he came to show them that their debt to God had been fully pardoned (2 Co 8:9; Mt 18:23-27).

THE PROCLAMATION OF REPENTANCE

Before he preached the gospel to the poor he had first to cry "REPENT!" (Mk 1:14-15). This strong word awakened in many deep contrition and remorse. Broken-hearted in sorrow for their sin they craved the mercy of God. But to cure the distracted conscience was the purpose for which Christ was sent by God (Jn 14:1,18; 2 Co 1:3-4; Mt 5:4).

Notice also the emphatic "he has sent me". Others may preach the gospel to the poor, others may say "repent", others may arouse deep conviction of sin, but only in Christ can the healing balm be found (Mt 11:29-30).

ANOINTED TO PREACH DELIVERANCE

Christ came to accomplish a three-fold deliverance –. . ..

DELIVERANCE TO THE CAPTIVES

Deliverance! Freedom! Release from all captivity by sin and Satan! Isaiah expressed it as *"opening the prison to those who are bound"* (Is 61:1). Paul, following the psalmist, said *"(Christ) ascended up on high, he led captivity captive"* (Ep 4:8; Ps 68:18). And again the great apostle exulted, *"He has delivered us from the power of darkness and has translated us into the kingdom of his beloved Son"* (Cl 1:1-13).

Changed from sin to righteousness, from defeat to victory, from fear to faith, from hell to heaven, from poverty to riches, from weakness to strength!

So the gospel Christ preached offered freedom from every imprisoning work of Satan, deliverance from the snare of every habit and sin, and release from every fear, defeat, or bondage!

RECOVERING OF SIGHT TO THE BLIND

The best comment on the meaning of this mighty act of deliverance is found in the Lord's commission to Paul –

> *I send you to the Gentiles, to open their eyes, so that they may turn from darkness to light, and from the power of Satan to God. Then they will receive pardon for their sin, and the right to stand among those who are sanctified by faith in me. (Ac 26:18).*

LIBERTY TO THOSE WHO ARE OPPRESSED

Liberty! Victory! Life! Escape from every heavy bruising blow of Satan!

The Greek word for *"oppressed"* means *"to crush, to shatter into small fragments"*.

This is its only occurrence in the New Testament, so we cannot compare it with another text to confirm its meaning. But the expression may surely be taken to include physical burdens, such as the crushing blows of failure and disease, of suffering and sickness. The Greeks used the word to describe someone who had been broken by calamity, or crushed by cruel oppression. Certainly, John's later promise of *"prosperity"* and *"health"* implies that people who are bruised by disease or shattered by poverty have a right to claim freedom.

The original prophecy quoted by Christ is found in *Isaiah* (61:1), which expresses the promise as, *"liberty to the captives"*. Some however, think that Christ was referring to an earlier prophecy (58:6): *"to break off the fetters of iniquity, to untie the traces of every yoke, to bring freedom to all who are oppressed, and to cast aside every yoke!"*

Sin is included there. But is not sickness also? Jesus plainly showed that sickness was a foul work of the wicked one. And is it not also a heavy burden, a bruising oppression, a galling yoke? So heavy and crushing and bitter is the yoke of disease, people spare no effort nor cost to throw it off and regain their health. Who among us considers sickness a pleasant thing? Who among us accepts it as a blessing from God? Who among us thanks him for it, making no attempt whatever to recover strength and freedom?

But we are left in no doubt about the real meaning of this great gospel of deliverance, preached by the Lord Jesus Christ. His actions reveal beyond argument the meaning of his words; for when he preached he also vigorously and continually healed the sick, all the sick, of all manner of sickness. Thus he set at liberty those who were bruised and brought deliverance to the captives.

ANOINTED TO PREACH THE ACCEPTABLE YEAR

The allusion here is to the year of jubilee, which occurred every fifty years in ancient Israel (see Le 25:9-41). Under that wonderful old law (which, because of human avariciousness, was rarely practised; compare Ne 5:1-13; Je 34:8-22) debtors were set at liberty, slaves were emancipated, homes and property were returned to those who had been compelled to mortgage them. This was indeed an *"acceptable"* year to those who had fallen into poverty, or bondage. It was a year of glad release; it brought freedom and a new beginning to the whole land.

The year of jubilee has now found its prophetic fulfilment in Christ. Now to us the profuse bounty of the Lord is offered, to us liberty has come, to us Christ has restored all that Satan, our task-master, extracted from us – our righteousness, our strength, our fellowship with God, our authority, our health, our hope, our happiness, our life!

CONCLUSION

Christ was expressly anointed by God and endowed by the Holy Spirit with power, for the specific task of preaching the tremendous gospel – good tidings to the poor, healing to the broken-hearted, deliverance to the captives, and the acceptable year of the Lord. Who dares to say that Christ is no longer filled with all the fulness of God? Who dares to say that the content of his gospel has changed, that his announced message and ministry is no longer valid?

God forbid!

As long as Christ has the words of God and the Holy Spirit without measure (Jn 3:34), and as long as there are people who are poor, broken-hearted, captive, blind, and bruised, the gospel of God's glorious jubilee, his acceptable year of release and restoration, should continue to sound joyfully among the nations (Ps 89:15-17).

HEALING IN THE ATONEMENT

Proof that healing of sickness, in addition to pardon of sin, was secured for us by Christ at Calvary, can be established in the following ways –

THE COVENANT RATIFIED AT THE CROSS

Since the New Covenant between God and man was finalised by Christ at Calvary (Lu 22:20; He 8:8; 9:15; etc.), and since one of the Redeemer's titles under this covenant is *Yahweh-Rapha*, it is plain that healing is one of the promised blessings of the atonement. In other words, if the healing promise is a valid part of the covenant, and if the covenant depends upon the cross for its ratification, then healing as well as pardon was wrought for us at Calvary.

An example of that can be found in an event from Israel's history. When the Israelites looked at the brazen serpent, they were at once healed of the deadly venom that had slain thousands of them (Nu 21:5-9). But notice, this incident was the only one from the whole Old Testament cited by Jesus as illustrative of the cross (Jn 3:14-17), which inescapably links the restorative power of the brass serpent to Calvary. May we not then conclude that those who gaze trustfully upon the cross today can be both pardoned and healed, as they were, who looked at the serpent?

Do you suppose the cross of Christ has less efficacy than a brass snake? Surely it is vastly more powerful!

The brass effigy brought only temporary pardon and transient healing, whereas Calvary contains a promise of total and eternal deliverance!

PARDON AND HEALING COMBINED

In the NT the same Greek words are used interchangeably to describe both *pardon* and *healing*, which clearly reveals the double nature of God's promise. The song of the Old Testament obviously sounds with sweeter melody in the New – *"Bless the Lord, O my soul, who forgives all your iniquity, who heals all your diseases!"* (Ps 103:1-3).

Salvation, in the New Testament use of the term, is undeniably all-embracing: it includes body, soul, and spirit; it brings both spiritual and physical health. Or perhaps I should say simply that the gospel offers *health* – health for the whole person. After all, Christ did not die just for your *body*, nor for your *soul* – he died for YOU! A body without a soul is not human; a soul without a body is not human. It requires body, soul, and spirit, blended together in a unified personality, to make a human being; and it is for that *whole person* Christ died on the cross.

That truth is established by the use of the following Greek words –

SOZO

– "to save, deliver, protect", both literally and figuratively. In the New Testament *sozo* is used to describe –

a) Physical healing

See Mt 9:21,22; Mk 5:23,28,34; 6:56; 10:52; Lu 8:36,48,50; 17:19; 18:42; Ac 4:9; 14:9; etc.

b) Spiritual salvation

See Mt 1:21; 18:11; Mk 16:16; Jn 12:47; Ro 11:14; 1 Co 1:21; 1 Ti 1:15; He 7:25; Ja 1:21; etc.

c) Physical and spiritual healing together

See Lu.9:56; Ja 5:15 ("save").

SOTERIA

– "deliverance, salvation, safety, "both physically and morally.

a) Physical deliverance

See Ac 27:34 ("strength"); Lu 1:71 ("saved").

b) Spiritual deliverance

See Ac 4:12; 28:28; Ro 10:10; etc.

DIASOZO

– "to save thoroughly, to cure, preserve, rescue"

a) Physical deliverance

See Lu 7:3 ("heal"); Mt 14:36 ("made well"); Ac 23:24 ("safe"); 27:43 ("save"); etc.

b) Spiritual deliverance

See 1 Pe 3:20 ("saved").

IAOMAI

– "to cure"

a) Physical healing

See Mt 8:8,13; 15:28; Lu 5:17; 6:19; 9:2; Jn 4:47.

b) Spiritual healing

See Mt 13:15 ("heal"); Jn 12:40; Ac 28:27; He 12:13.

c) Both together

See Lu 4:18; Ac 10:38; Ja 5:16; 1 Pe 2:24 ("healed").

The free use of those four Greek words to describe both spiritual salvation and physical healing, shows that the apostles viewed both benefits as a result of the one act of Christ. To quote Peter in the last reference listed above, *"He himself bore our sins in his body on the tree . . . By his wounds you have been healed."* On the cross, and for all who are willing to believe, Christ secured a double salvation: healing of both **soul** and **body**.

CHRIST IS SAVIOUR AND HEALER

Passages where pardon and healing are linked together clearly show that both benefits can be found in the cross –

1) Matthew 9:1-8

The scribes accused Jesus of blasphemy because he claimed the right to forgive sins, but they did not deny his healing ministry. Today the position is reversed: people accept that Christ is able to *pardon*, but they often become offended when we say he will also *heal*!

Jesus said that his healing ministry was proof of his ability to pardon. We might say today that his pardoning ministry is proof of his ability to heal! The act of forgiveness is a vastly greater work than the act of healing. If Christ can pardon he can heal. Surely the lesser work is contained in the greater!

When the superb feat of reconciliation was accomplished at Calvary so also, as a natural result, was the work of divine deliverance.

2) Matthew 10:7-8

When he commissioned his disciples, here and in several other places, Christ linked the command to preach the gospel with a command to heal the sick, thus pungently demonstrating that healing was one of the benefits people gained when they embraced the gospel.

3) Luke 7:50; 18:42

To the woman who was a sinner Jesus said, *"Your faith has saved you!"* To the man who was blind Jesus said, *"Your faith has made you well!"* But in the Greek text the two statements are word for word the same. There is no difference between the word of Christ that brought a sinner pardon and the word that brought a sick person healing. Some interesting conclusions can be drawn –

a)   The faith that brings salvation is the same faith that brings healing. There is no difference between the faith that believes in Christ as Saviour and the faith that believes in him as Healer. Just as we must believe the gospel of pardon to be saved, so must we believe the gospel of deliverance to be healed. By faith we receive Christ as Redeemer, by faith we receive him as Great Physician.

b)   The salvation that brings pardon, reconciliation and peace, by faith, is exactly the same as the salvation that brings healing, abundant life, and deliverance, by faith. If we are bound by sin, the gospel offers pardon and victory. If we are gripped by sickness, the gospel offers healing and abundant life. If we are troubled by guilt, and we come trustingly to Christ, he will say to us as he said to the woman, *"Your faith has saved you, go in peace!"* If we are afflicted by disease and we come trustingly to Christ, he will say to us as he said to the blind man, *"Receive your healing: your faith has made you whole!"*

c)   Obviously then, Christ is willing to respond to faith equally, in giving either *pardon* or *healing*. The whole ministry of Jesus shows that God sees these two as twin gifts, which are available to all who believe the gospel of Christ. "Salvation" then, means deliverance from both *sin* and *sickness*. If we accept Christ as Saviour we should also see in him our Healer. If we accept him as Healer we should also see in him our Saviour. By faith in Christ we can be saved – saved from sin and saved from sickness.

d) The blind man, after his sight was restored, at once began to follow Christ and to glorify God, thus indicating that spiritual salvation had also come to him. The faith that saved him brought him both pardon and healing.

4) John 3:14

As we have already seen (*Healing in the Old Testament*), the incident of the Brazen Serpent links both pardon and healing together in the redemptive work of Christ.

5) Acts 10:38; 1 John 3:8

These, and similar texts, embrace the entire public ministry of Christ, culminating in his death and resurrection. Since his public ministry included both pardon and healing, and since these texts sum up the significance of his life and death for us today, it is plain that we too can claim both forgiveness and deliverance.

6) John 5:8-14

Having healed the man, Christ said, *"See, you are well!"* Not just well physically, but also spiritually – for the Master's next words show that the healing of the man's body extended also to his soul: *"Sin no more, otherwise something worse may befall you."*

7) Mark 5:34

"Jesus said to her, 'Daughter, your faith has made you well.'" The word translated "well" is *sozo*, which I have already shown embraces both spiritual and physical healing. Christ leaves no doubt that this double healing did come to the woman; for he continued, *"Go in peace, and be cured of your disease."* So here is another case where one act of faith in the Lord Jesus Christ brought the double benefit of full salvation and complete healing.

CHAPTER EIGHT:

THE WOUNDED PHYSICIAN

He healed them all – the blind, the lame, the palsied,
The sick in body and the weak in mind,
Whoever came, no matter how afflicted,
Were sure a sov'reign remedy to find.

His word gave health, his touch restored the vigour
To every weary pain-exhausted frame;
And all he asked before he gave the blessing
Was simple faith in him from those who came. [15]

"Christ himself bore our sins in his body on the tree . . . by his wounds you have been healed" (1 Pe 2:24).

T he word *"healed"* in the original Greek is *iaomai*, which means *"to cure a sickness"*. What is its sense here? Literal or figurative? Spiritual or physical? Or both? An examination of its use in the NT shows –

- It is used 21 times to describe plain physical healing – as, for example, in Mt 8:8,13.

- It is used once (Ac 10:38) to describe both physical and spiritual deliverance.

- It is used five times in a figurative sense to describe moral and spiritual cure – but in these cases it still retains its primary meaning, for physical cure is made a type or symbol of spiritual restoration (Mt 13:15; Lu 4:18; Jn 12:40; Ac 28:27; He 12:13).

---

(15) Anonymous.

- Two derivatives of *iaomai* are used in the following verses, describing physical healing alone – Lu 13:32; Ac 4:22,30 (*iasis*); and 1 Co 12:9,28,30 (*iama*).

- The final use of the word in the NT is our text (1 Pe 2:24).

It can be seen that the overwhelming meaning of *iaomai* is bodily cure, and that it refers to spiritual well-being only when it is deliberately used in a figurative sense. Yet there is no indication in our text that Peter was using the word symbolically. He appears rather to be stating sober fact: *"By his wounds you have been healed."* I can see no good reason to doubt that Peter carefully chose to use *iaomai* here in order to avoid ambiguity – he intended to say that physical healing was obtained for us at Calvary.

If it is true that we can obtain pardon because *"he himself bore our sins in his body on the cross"*, then it is also true that we can obtain cure of our sickness because *"by his wounds we have been healed"*.

This literal meaning of Peter's words is borne out by considering the original context in *Isaiah* – *"with his stripes we are healed"* (53:5). The Hebrew word for *"healed"* is *rapha*, which is the word God compounded with his own name (*Yahweh*) when he made his covenant of physical healing with Israel (Ex 15:26; *"I am the Lord, your healer"* – *Yahweh-Rapha*).

In the OT *rapha* is used many times, sometimes describing *physical cure*, but other times in a figurative sense, to describe *spiritual restoration*. But the basic meaning of the word remains physical *"mending"*, being *"made well"*. Even when *rapha* is used in a spiritual sense, we know from God's covenant with Israel that physical benefit was to follow this spiritual restoration.

There is an arresting contrast in the grammatical tenses used by Isaiah and Peter. The prophet said, *"are healed"*; but the apostle wrote, *"were healed"*. Isaiah used the prophetic present tense, for he was looking forward to a work that was yet to be accomplished. But Peter used the aorist tense, because he was looking back to a work that had been completed. Peter is saying, in effect, that healing is now your perfect right; it is already reserved for you under your name; all you need to do is to claim what is already yours, to lay hold of it by faith.

CARRIED RIGHT AWAY

In the prophecy just referred to, Isaiah also declared, *"Surely he took upon himself our infirmities and carried away our pains"* (vs. 4). Matthew obviously thought those words contained a prediction that the Messiah would heal the sick, for he quoted them in direct connection with Jesus' healing ministry – Mt 8:16-17. Notice –

1) Isaiah clearly showed the two great benefits that would come from the atoning death of Christ. Not only was he *"wounded for our transgressions"* he also *"took upon himself our infirmities"*; not only was he *"bruised for our iniquities"*, he also *"carried away our pains"*; not only was *"the flogging that brought us peace laid upon him"*, but also, *"by his wounds we are healed."* Who can doubt then that Jesus, on the cross, secured both forgiveness of every sin and healing of every sickness.

2) It cannot be said that the prophecy of healing was limited to the time of Jesus' earthly ministry, and only the prophecy of pardon belongs to our time, for both predictions are inextricably bound together. Note also that the passage in *1 Peter 2:24* is a summary of the words of Isaiah, in which Peter applies both aspects of the prophecy to the church: he bore our sins on the cross, and also wrought healing for our bodies.

3) Some have suggested that the words *"borne"*, and *"carried"* [16] (as used by Isaiah), mean only that the Messiah, when he came, would through his sufferings enter into a sympathetic sharing of our sorrows. Therefore we may now expect him to stand by us and help carry the burden – but he will not actually remove it from us. That is easily disproved –

a) The Hebrew word for *"borne"* means to *"lift up"*. Exactly the same word is used in the twelfth verse, *"he bore the sin of many."* When applied to sin, every Christian knows that *"bore"* means to lift up and take right away. When applied to our *"griefs"* it must mean the same: That Christ has borne them all away. If we can believe that Christ has carried our sins away, we find peace with God. Likewise, if we can

---

(16) I am reverting here to the language of the KJV.

believe that Christ has carried our griefs away, we find healing from God.

b) The Hebrew word for *"carried"* is used also in the eleventh verse, *"he shall bear their iniquities."* Once again the real meaning of the word is obvious. Only because he has carried our sins right away can God's *"righteous Servant justify many"*. And because he also carried away our sorrows; he can just as readily heal all who trust in him.

c) This was confirmed by Matthew when he quoted Isaiah. He used two Greek words that are translated (in the RSV) as *"took"* and *"bore"*. The word translated *"took"* means *"to get hold of"*. It is used, for example, in Mt 16:9,10; 25:1,3,4; Mk 14:22,23; Jn 19:27; Ph 2:7; etc; and its meaning is plain – *"to pick up and take away"*. The word translated *"bore"* means *"to lift up and remove"*. It is translated *"bear"*, *"carry"*, *"take up"*; see Mt 3:11; Lu 14:27; etc. Once again the meaning is plain: Jesus took hold of our diseases, lifted them up, and carried them away.

4) The original words translated respectively *"griefs"*, *"sorrows"*, *"infirmities"*, *"diseases"*, all refer to physical illness –

a) **Griefs** – the Hebrew word means *"malady"*, *"anxiety"*, *"calamity"*. It comes from another root word, which means *"to be weak, sick, or afflicted"*. In our Bibles it is translated, *"disease"*, *"grief"*, *"sick"*, *"sickness"*; etc.

b) **Sorrows** – the Hebrew word means *"anguish"* or *"affliction"*; and it comes from another root word, which means *"to feel pain"*. In our Bibles it is translated *"grief"*, *"pain,"* *"sorrow"*; etc.

c) **Infirmities** – the Greek word means "feebleness of body or mind", "malady". It is translated, "disease" "infirmity" "sickness" "weakness" – see for example, Lu 5:15; 8:2.

d) **Diseases** – the Greek word means *"a malady"*; and it is translated *"disease"*, *"infirmity"*, *"sickness"* – see for example, Mt 4:23; Lu 7:21; Ac 19:12.

5) The implication of the prophecy of Isaiah is therefore unmistakable: not only would Christ carry away the **sins** of his people, he would also

remove their *diseases*. In his atoning death at Calvary the Lord provided deliverance from both the infirmity of sin and the grief of sickness.

THE CURSE OF THE LAW

One of the most startling declarations in the whole Bible was written by Paul –

> *Christ redeemed us from the curse of the law, having become a curse for us; for it is written, Cursed is everyone who hangs on a tree (Ga 3:13; De 21:23).*

The curse of the law was three-fold –

1) Those who broke God's commandment became enmeshed in the tyrannical power of sin, and were not able to escape (Ro 7:5,15; 2 Pe 2:19; Ro 6:16; Pr 5:22; Jn 8:34).

2) Death passed upon all who sinned, both physical death and spiritual death, resulting in everlasting banishment from the presence of God (Ro 5:12; 6:23; Ez 18:4,20; Re 20:12-15).

3) Associated with death was the curse of sickness, pain, and suffering (De 28:15-22,27-29,35,45,58-61; etc.)

But Christ has redeemed us from that curse through his death on the cross, for the scripture says that a man who has been sentenced to death by hanging on a tree is accursed of God. But the curse applies only to those who have *"committed a sin worthy of death"*, and so are justly executed. How then can it affect Jesus, for he was without sin? (Jn 8:46; 14:30; 18:38; 7:45-46; 2 Co 5:21; He 4:15)

Christ was cursed by God only because our sins were laid upon him on the cross. He became guilty with all our guilt. In fact, he was made sin for us (2 Co 5:21; 1 Pe 3:18; Is 53:12; He 9:28; 1 Jn 3:5). Bearing in his body on the tree all the sin of each of us, he became infected with the full curse that should have fallen upon us (Is 53:3-4).

The prophet said,

> *His appearance was so marred beyond human resemblance, and his form beyond that of the sons of men (Is 52:14).*

And again,

The ploughers ploughed upon my back: they made long their furrows (Ps 129:3)

And again,

All thy waves and thy billows have gone over me . . . Insults have broken my heart so that I am in despair. I looked for pity, but there was none; and for comforters, but I found none. They gave me poison for food, and for my thirst they gave me vinegar to drink (Ps 42:7; 69:20-21).

And again,

I gave my back to the smiters, and my cheeks to those who pulled out the beard; I hid not my face from shame and spitting (Is 50:6).

Jesus bore the curse for us.

In so doing, he redeemed us. He paid the ransom price; he rescued us from the poverty, shame, slavery, and death into which our own sin had placed us. By his death on the cross he purchased our freedom from the curse, the whole curse, of the broken law. Now we may claim victory over sin (Ro 6:6,14,18,22-23); we may claim healing of every sickness and disease (Jn 10:10; Mk 16:18; Ja 5:14-15).

We who believe are loosed from death, for we have passed from death to life (Jn 5:24; He 2:14-15; 1 Jn 5:11-13). The physical healing we claim now, on the basis of the atonement, is simply a foretaste of that greater and eternal victory over the grave that has been made ours in Christ.

CHAPTER NINE:

THE HEALING COMMISSION

Dearest Lord, may I see you today
And every day in the person of your sick,
And, whilst nursing them, minister unto you.
Though you hide yourself behind the unattractive
Disguise of the irritable, the exacting, the unreasonable,
May I still recognize you, and say,
"Jesus, my patient, how sweet it is to serve you." [17]

As soon as he had gathered together a band of disciples Jesus commanded them to follow exactly in his footsteps by preaching the gospel, healing the sick, and casting out demons. That commission is found in the following places –

COMMANDED TO HEAL

MATTHEW 9:35 – 10:1-8

Just as Jesus had healed *"every disease and every sickness"*, so too the disciples were to go and heal *"every disease and every sickness"*. And the reason behind this commission was the same as the reason that stood behind Jesus' healing ministry. The Lord himself healed the sick primarily because they had need of healing (Lu 9:11), and because he had deep compassion for their sufferings (Mt 14:14). That same need and that same compassion impelled him to send his disciples on the same mission.

---

(17) Mother Teresa (1910-97), Albanian-born Roman Catholic missionary. A Gift for God: "Love to Pray" (1975). From The Columbia Dictionary of Quotations, Columbia University Press, 1995.

The multitudes are still fainting, the compassion of Christ is certainly as great today as it was then; we can only conclude that his present disciples are under command to do the same work – preach the gospel and heal the sick.

MARK 6:7,12-13

This passage is the same as that in Matthew, except that here we have a record of the successful accomplishment of the Lord's commission. Notice, though, the contrast between the disciples and Christ –

- they were sent out in pairs so that each might encourage the faith and zeal of the other; also

- their ministry was apparently more limited than Christ's; they found it necessary to anoint with oil; and

- whereas Christ healed *"multitudes"* and *"all"*, the disciples healed only *"many"*.

Nonetheless, it is wonderful to see this band of humble men going out in the strength of the Lord's command, preaching the gospel, and in his name healing the sick and casting out demons.

There is no reason why we should not do the same.

Those twelve were only men –

- they were not especially holy (Judas was included amongst them)

- there were many short-comings in their understanding and outlook (Mt 15:16; Jn 14:9; Lu 24:25; 22:24)

- they were not always successful in healing the sick (Mt 17:16).

But despite such faults they brought salvation and healing to large numbers of people. The church today should surely be able at least to equal their efforts!

MARK 9:38-40; LUKE 9:49-50

This stranger is one of the most remarkable men in the Bible. He apparently did not have any personal contact with Jesus, and had not received a direct command to heal the sick; yet he understood two vital things –

a) that simple compassion was the real motivation behind the healing commission the Lord had given his disciples.

Christ healed the sick because they needed healing, and he expected his disciples to follow the example he had set. Compassion is not a special prerogative of specially chosen people; it should be shared by all who claim to serve Christ. And if we share his compassion we should share his response to it.

Then the stranger understood also –

b) that the name of Jesus has power and authority over demons and disease, not only when it is spoken by apostles and preachers, but when it is spoken by anyone who believes in Christ.

Whoever that stranger was, he had grasped a principle of the kingdom of God that only he and Jesus understood at that time. He realised that God has given authority to all his servants to heal the sick in Jesus' name. Therefore he asked no-one's permission, he desired no personal word from Christ, he sought no vision nor any special divine visitation; he simply went out in faith, knowing the love of God and the need of men, and in the name of Christ he set the captives free!

The stranger actually showed a greater understanding of the will of Christ than the beloved apostle John. Christ rebuked John when he complained that the man was not a member of their group. Jesus declared that the man, although he was a stranger, was acting with them, not against them, and that he was serving the best interests of the kingdom of God. And when the Lord said, *"Do not prevent him!"* he gave an open invitation to his disciples everywhere to show the same faith and enterprise.

LUKE 9:1-2,6

Is there any Christian who would deny that we are still under command to go to every town and place preaching the gospel? Then how can it be denied that we ought also to *"heal everywhere?"*

There is not one sentence in the whole Bible to show that while the command to *preach* is still valid the command to *heal* has been abrogated! Unbelief alone has caused the second part of the Lord's commission to be forgotten.

LUKE 10:1,9,17-19

Following on from commissioning the twelve (Lu 9:1) and the incident of the stranger (vs. 49), Christ now commissioned seventy-two [18] other disciples to preach and to heal. These men (and possibly women also) found that they too, as they obeyed the Lord's command and exercised faith in the immense power of his name, could do as Jesus had done. The sick were healed, demons were cast out, and they returned with great joy.

Now, some people feel compelled to look upon the twelve apostles as men of special calibre (although there is no indication of it in the scripture). Hence they argue that while the *apostles* had power to heal the sick in Jesus' name, *we* cannot hope to copy them. But then, what about this larger group of disciples? They were just people who were close followers of Christ, who were near him when he desired to broaden the scope of his ministry. It is inconceivable that they were all paragons of holiness, virtue, or faith, or were significantly different from any other group of loyal followers of Jesus. Therefore, if *they* could heal the sick in his name, then so may *we*.

Why 72 disciples? Jesus was probably showing that the mission of the 72 was symbolical of a world-wide healing mandate. This is because the Jews, using the LXX version of the *Table of Nations* (Ge 10), argued that there were just 72 nations in the world. Thus among the rabbis "72" became a symbol for the whole world. The Church Fathers, copying the rabbis, held to a similar opinion –

> Many historians say that there are 75 nations and tongues . . . (but) according to the true reckoning, there appear to be 72 generic dialects, as our scriptures hand down" (Clement of Alexandria, c. 200; *Misc. Bk. I, Ch. 21*)

> Every nation has an angel, to whom God has committed the government of that nation . . . For the Most High God, who alone holds the power of all things, has divided all the nations of the earth into 72 parts, and over

---

(18) Some Greek manuscripts have 70, some 72. The latter is the better reading.

those he has appointed angels as princes. (Anon. c. 250; the *Recognitions of Clement, Bk. II, Ch. 42*)

From (the sons of Noah) the islands of nations were dispersed on the earth after the flood. Hence we gather that there were at that time 73 nations (or rather, as will be shown later, 72) . . . Let us therefore search among those early peoples of mankind who were, we gather, divided into 72 nations and as many languages. (Augustine of Hippo, c. 400; *City of God, 16.3&9*)

Likewise, an anonymous 4th century work, *The Tiburtine Sibyl*, contains a prophecy that was supposedly given before the birth of Christ. It reads like a garbled version of *Luke 10:1*, and it shows that the early church understood the world-wide ramifications of Jesus' action in appointing just 72 disciples –

And he (Jesus) will take men from Galilee, and will give laws, and he will say to them, "The word which you have received from me, preach it to the people of the 72 languages." (From the *Oracle of Baalbek*)

So when Jesus appointed 72 people it was a symbolic way of saying that their ministry of salvation and healing belonged not just to Palestine, but to the whole world. In this connection, Luke's saying about *"every town and place where he was to go"* takes on a larger spiritual meaning: that is, it belonged not just to a short period before Calvary, but reaches across the years to *"every place"* where the Spirit of God intends to move.

Once again, note that the 72 were just people whose names were written down in heaven! (Lu 10:20). Is your name written down in the Lamb's book of life? Then the command Jesus gave them is given also to you! You too can take power and authority over all of Satan's works, you can cast out demons, you can *"tread on serpents and scorpions"*, and in his name you can *"cure diseases"*!

If you can get people to listen to you when you testify, if you can get them to believe the gospel promise, if you can create in them faith in Christ as Saviour and Physician, then his name on your lips can bring them pardon and healing just as effectively as if you were one of the seventy-two, or even one of the twelve.

JOHN 14:12-14

Nothing could be plainer than those words of Christ. He gave to his disciples an incredible promise. We learn –

It was spoken not just to the people present at the time, but to all Christians everywhere – *"everyone who believes in me."*

The promise is that we should do the works Christ was doing. What was he doing? The answer is clear – he was preaching, and especially, he was healing the sick and casting out demons! Those same works, the Lord said, we also can and should do. It is not possible to escape that plain meaning., Jesus could hardly have meant to exclude his healing ministry when he said that we, if we believe, can do what he did. None of his other public works were so prominent nor so constant. How can we escape taking him to mean that we too should be active, as he was, in healing the sick and casting out demons?

Still further, he said that we should do *"greater works"* than he performed. Not greater in quality, for that is not possible (Mt 10:24-25a), but greater in quantity, [19] because the personal ministry of Christ was soon to be cut short by his return to his Father. The ministry of Jesus was abundant, in fact it was superb, and no one man in the space of a mere three years could even begin to equal its fantastic scope and accomplishment. But over a period of many years' service the church collectively should bring healing to a multitude of people, far surpassing in number those healed by Christ.

We can gain the faith and spiritual authority we need for this ministry, by prayer. In this we have the example of the Lord himself, for he frequently went aside to pray, sometimes for a whole night (Mt 14:23; Mk 6:46; Lu 6:12; 9:28).

---

(19) Perhaps better, the *"greater"* work may be the one thing the church can do that Jesus of Nazareth could not do (since the Day of Pentecost had not yet come), that is, we can impart Holy Spirit baptism by the laying on of hands. The larger context of *John 14, 15, & 16* (where there are several references to the coming outpouring of the Spirit, which occurred on the Day of Pentecost), suggests that this is actually what Jesus had in mind.

Our authority, both in prayer and in working the works of Christ, is found in the name of Jesus. His name used with confidence in its power, will bring perfect freedom to those who are bound, and will give the believer instant access into the presence of God.

The actual "worker" is still Christ: *"whatever you ask I will do!"* We pray for the sick in his name; but it is his hand that sets them free. Thus no person is wrongfully honoured, but *"the Father is glorified through the Son"*.

The scope of this promise is as broad as human need *"Whatever you ask, I will do it!"* The only qualification is that we ask *"in his name"*, and *"that the Father may be glorified through the Son"*; which precludes us from asking for anything that would dishonour the name of Jesus or detract from the glory of God.

The Master's next word was, *"If you love me, you will heed my commands"* (vs. 15). Do we love him? Then we should heed his commands by setting ourselves to pray, to learn the authority of the name of Jesus, to believe, and to do the works that he did! [20]

MATTHEW 28:19-20

There is no dispute among Christians concerning the first two parts of the Lord's command – all are agreed that the church is obligated to preach the gospel and baptise converts. But then the Lord laid down a third injunction: *"teach them to obey everything I have commanded you!"* Did the Lord command the disciples to heal the sick and cast out demons? Then they were to teach others to fulfil the same instruction! And this command to continue in every instruction that the Lord gave to his first disciples extends to *"all nations"* and to all believers until *"the close of the age"*.

---

(20) I am speaking collectively here, of the church. Individually, we each have our own calling in Christ, which may or may not confront us with a need to bring healing to the sick. But wherever a local church is found, functioning as the body of Christ in its community, then a power of healing should be flowing through it.

CHAPTER TEN:

THE ACTS OF THE APOSTLES

O Son of Man, to right my lot
  Nought but thy presence can avail;
Yet on the road thy wheels are not,
  Nor on the sea thy sail.
My fancied ways why should'st thou heed?
  Thou com'st down thine own secret stair,
Com'st down to answer all my need,
  Yea, every bygone prayer! [21]

T he early disciples eagerly embraced the commission Christ gave them to preach and to heal, and the book of *Acts* contains a thrilling description of the many signs and wonders that followed their ministry. Here is a summary of Luke's record –

MIRACLES IN THE BOOK OF ACTS

The incredible story began with the miracle of glossolalia on the day of Pentecost (2:1-4); and it continued with *"many wonders and signs being done by the apostles"*, so that the whole city fell into a reverent fear of God and of his servants (2:43). The story of the early church then continues in a blaze of the supernatural –

- A man who had been crippled for forty years (4:22) was healed by Peter and John (3:1-16), resulting in the addition of several thousand people to the church (4:4).

- Superb wisdom and authority were given to the disciples (4:13,16; and cp. Lu 21:15).

---

(21) George McDonald (1824-1905).

- The disciples prayed that they might have yet greater boldness to preach the word, and that God would stretch out his hand to work signs and wonders (4:29-30).

- The building where they prayed was shaken by God and they were filled with the Holy Spirit (4:31).

- Great power and great grace was with them (4:33).

- Ananias and Sapphira were struck dead by the judgment of Peter, and deep fear came upon them all (5:1-11).

- *"Many signs and wonders were performed among the people by the hands of the apostles . . . and an ever-increasing number of believers were added to the Lord, crowds of both of men and women"* (5:12-14).

- *"They even carried out the sick, putting them on the footpath on beds and pallets . . . including those who were troubled by unclean spirits, and they were all healed"* (5:15-16).

- The apostles were released from prison by the angel of the Lord (5:17-19).

- Then Stephen,

  full of grace and power, performed amazing miracles and signs among the people (6:8).

- Philip preached in Samaria and

  the crowd was unanimous in accepting what Philip said when he preached to them, especially when they saw the miracles he performed – for unclean spirits, screaming aloud, came out of many who were possessed by them, and many other paralysed and lame folk were healed (8:5-8).

- Philip was supernaturally transported by the Holy Spirit (8:39-40).

- Saul was stricken blind by God, converted, and healed by Ananias (9:1-18).

- Peter healed Aeneas who had been paralysed and bedfast for eight years (9:32-43) so that a whole town was converted (vs. 35).

- Peter raised Dorcas from the dead and many more believed on the Lord (9:36-42).

- Cornelius and his household were filled with the Holy Spirit and spoke in other tongues (10:44-46), a repetition of the Pentecostal event that occurred also in other places.

- Some disciples from Cyprus and Cyrene went to Antioch and there preached the gospel, *"and the hand of the Lord was with them so that a great number believed and turned to the Lord"* (11:20-21). Barnabas also, *"a good man, full of the Holy Spirit and of faith"*, came to Antioch and again *"a great number of people were added to the Lord"* (vs. 24).

The language used in those references, when it is compared with earlier passages, where the same terminology is used in a setting of *"signs, wonders, and miracles"*, implies that the success of the church at Antioch was largely attributable (as it was elsewhere) to a rich occurrence of the supernatural.

- Peter was released from prison by an angel (12:1-11).

- Herod was stricken by the angel of the Lord *"because he failed to give glory to God"*, so he suffered the penalty and *"was eaten by worms"* (12:23).

- Paul caused Elymas the sorcerer to be stricken blind, which resulted in the salvation of the Roman deputy (13:9-12).

- Paul and Barnabas preached at Iconium for a long time and the Lord *"confirmed his gracious message by enabling the apostles to work signs and wonders among the people"* (14:3).

- At Lystra Paul healed a crippled man (14:7-10). But notice, this man *"had faith to be healed"*. The same comment could probably have been added by Luke to many other places where miracles of healing occurred. It is not unusual for the biblical writers to draw occasional attention to something that they assume their readers will add to every similar account.

- Paul, having been brutally stoned, was miraculously restored when the disciples stood around and prayed for him (14:19-21).

- Paul and Barnabas spoke in Jerusalem of the *"signs and wonders God had done through them among the Gentiles"* (15:12).

- At Philippi Paul delivered a girl who was tormented by a spirit of divination (16:16-18).

- Paul and Silas were released from prison by an earthquake (16:25-26).

- A company of believers at Ephesus were filled with the Holy Spirit and spoke in tongues when Paul laid hands on them (19:6).

- *"God did extraordinary miracles by the hands of Paul. Pieces of cloth that he had touched were taken to sick people, and their diseases left them and evil spirits came out of them"* (10:11-12).

- Some false exorcists were soundly beaten, which caused the name of the Lord Jesus to be magnified, and the word of God mightily grew and prevailed (19:13-20).

- Paul raised a young man to life again (20:9-10).

- Paul remained unaffected by a viper's poison (28:1-6).

- Paul healed the father of Publius and many others also (28:7-9).

So we see that wherever they went, the first disciples (not only the apostles) preached the gospel, laid hands on the sick, and set themselves to cast out demons. And the Lord truly worked with them, confirming his word with following signs. There seems to be no valid reason, apart from unbelief, why the same pattern should not be fulfilled today.

THE WORD CONFIRMED

One of the basic values of *"signs, wonders, and miracles,"* is the power they have to confirm the truth of the word of God. Many passages present this important purpose of the healing ministry – [22]

---

(22) The cluster of verses that follow all come from the RSV.

- *"They went forth and preached everywhere, while the Lord worked with them and confirmed the message by the signs that attended it"* (Mk 16:20).

- *"Jesus of Nazareth was a man attested to you by God with mighty works and wonders and signs"* (Ac 2:22).

- *"Many wonders and signs were done through the apostles and fear came upon every soul"* (Ac 2:43).

- *"Grant to thy servants to speak thy words with all boldness, while thou stretchest out thy hand to heal, and signs and wonders are performed, through the name of thy holy servant Jesus"* (Ac 4:29-30).

- *"Many signs and wonders were done among the people by the hands of the apostles . . . and more than ever believers were added to the Lord, multitudes both of men and women"* (Ac 5:12,14).

- *"And the multitudes with one accord gave heed to what was said by Philip, when they heard him and saw the signs which he did"* (Ac 8:6).

- *"The Lord bore witness to the word of his grace, granting signs and wonders to be done by their hands"* (Ac 14:3).

- *"Christ has wrought through me to win obedience from the Gentiles, by word and deed, by the power of signs and wonders, by the power of the Holy Spirit, so that . . . I have fully preached the gospel of Christ"* (Ro 15:18-19).

- *"The signs of a true apostle were performed among you in all patience, with signs and wonders and mighty works"* (2 Co 12:12).

- *"(The word) was declared at first by the Lord, and it was attested to us by those who had heard him, while God also bore witness by signs and wonders and various miracles"* (He 2:4).

If the word of God and the preachers of the gospel needed to be established by signs, wonders, and miracles in Bible days, then the same need exists today. Nor is it reasonable to say that we have the witness of the Bible and therefore have no need of contemporary miracles. The early disciples could have pointed to the miracles of Jesus (Ac 2:22) as sufficient proof of the gospel; but they were not content to do so. They insisted that God should personally confirm his word through them (Ac 4:29-30).

Today we are removed from the biblical record by many centuries, and there are hundreds of preachers and multitudes of people who no longer believe in the accuracy or truth of the scriptures. If ever the word of God needed to be confirmed by signs following it is today!

Further, Christ himself set us an example. As I have already shown above, he was not content to tell the disciples of John the Baptist only about the miracles he had wrought before they came to him. Far from it! Right there in their presence he healed the sick and cast out demons. Only then did he say, *"Go and tell John what you have seen and heard: the blind receive their sight, the lame walk, lepers are cleansed, and the deaf hear, the dead are raised up, the poor have good news preached to them!"* (Lu 7:19-22, RSV).

I am convinced that without the attesting power of the signs, wonders, and miracles they kept on working in Jesus' name, the early disciples could not have fulfilled the mission Christ gave them. Nor can we.

CHAPTER ELEVEN:

IN HIS NAME

Jesus, the name high over all,
   In hell, or earth, or sky;
Angels and men before it fall
   And devils fear and fly.

Jesus! the name to sinners dear,
   The name to sinners given;
It scatters all their guilty fear,
   And turns their hell to heaven.

Jesus the prisoner's fetters breaks,
   And bruises Satan's head;
Power into strengthless souls he speaks,
   And life unto the dead! [23]

T he most fully described miracle in the book of Acts occurred at the Beautiful Gate of the temple, when Peter and John brought healing to a crippled man (Ac 3:1-16). Concerning this miracle note – [24]

OUR TRUE WEALTH

The true and greatest wealth of the church is found in the name of Jesus. How great is the contrast between Peter's words and the Lord's rebuke (only a few years later) of the church at Laodicea. Peter said, *"I have no*

---

(23) Charles Wesley.

(24) For more extended discussions on the power of Jesus' name, see the *VCC* books <u>Throne Rights</u>, <u>Faith Dynamics</u>, and <u>Mountain Movers</u>.

silver and gold". The Laodiceans boasted of their great wealth (Re 3:14-19); although in fact they were *"wretched, pitiable, poor, blind and naked"*.

On the other hand Peter, although he claimed no worldly wealth, did have the power of God through the name of Christ! He said, *"I give you what I have; in the name of Jesus Christ of Nazareth, walk!"*

He had the name of Jesus; and in that name there was power to bring healing to a crippled man.

Here is true wealth indeed!

Yet how many Christians are really aware of the awesome power God has vested in Jesus' name?

OUR TRUE POWER

POWER BY HIS NAME

The name of Jesus has great power because he who bears it is the Son of God (vs. 13); therefore all the fulness of the Godhead dwells in him (Cl 2:9). Behind his name stands the might of his deity.

When Peter said, *"In the name of Jesus Christ of Nazareth, walk,"* the authority of God was unleashed, and the crippled limbs had to obey: *"at once his feet and ankles were made strong, and leaping up he stood and began to walk!"* Later on Peter declared to the people, *"(Jesus') name, by faith in his name, has made this man strong . . . the faith which is through Jesus has given the man this perfect health in the presence of you all."*

Christ is the *"Holy One and the Just"*, and it was *"not possible for him to be held by the pangs of death"*, nor for him to be *"abandoned to Hades"*, nor for him to see corruption.

He is the Prince of Life, who, though he was *"killed by wicked men, was raised again by God"* (vs. 15). And now *"God has glorified his servant Jesus"* (vs. 13), so that he has been given *"a name so much above every other name, that at the name of Jesus every knee must bow, in heaven and on earth and under the earth"* (Ph 2:9-11).

At the sound of that mighty name, when it is spoken in faith, every work of Satan, every sickness, must yield, and one day even death itself will collapse before it (Jn 5:24-29).

SALVATION BY HIS NAME

Peter emphatically declared: *"By the name of Jesus Christ of Nazareth . . . this man now stands before you made whole . . . And salvation cannot be found anywhere else, for no other name under heaven has been granted to us upon which we must call if we would be saved"* (Ac 4:10-12).

The word *"salvation"* is *soteria*, which I have shown earlier means rescue, safety, deliverance, both physically and morally.

The word *"saved"* is *sozo*, which means to save, deliver, protect, whether literally or figuratively, physically or morally.

Peter applied those words primarily to the miracle of healing that had occurred in the cripple; but then he extended them to include the spiritual deliverance that had also been given to him – that is, the cripple had been restored both physically and spiritually.

The Christ who can *heal* in this way must also be powerful to *save*. The Christ who can effect such a great *salvation* must also be powerful to *heal*. Both blessings are ours through faith in his name.

Don't miss, either, the significance of Peter's statement that the crippled man was not healed because an *apostle* had prayed for him. His cure did not come because Peter and John were especially holy or had some unique power (Ac 3:12). This cripple was made whole *simply because two men had faith in the power of the name of Jesus.*

Peter said plainly, *"The name of Jesus, by faith in his name, has made this man strong"* (vs. 16).

I do not see how this conclusion can be avoided: if any of us have the same faith in the matchless name of Jesus as Peter and John had, then the same miracles can be wrought by us!

I must allow that possession of such faith, whether constantly or temporarily, is a gift of God, and that not all are privileged to receive the gift in the same measure (Ro 12:3b), or in the same strength on every occasion.

But there is still no biblical reason why any sincere Christian may not obtain at least some degree of dynamic faith in Jesus' name, and in the authority of that name conquer sickness and other satanic oppressions.

I am sure God is willing for us all to appropriate a much more vigorous faith than we actually do have. Very few of God's servants utilise more than a small part of the spiritual resources available to them in Christ.

OUR TRUE FAITH

1) This emphasis on acting in the name of Jesus, with an understanding of the power and authority the proper use of his name confers, is found in many places –

- *"In his name will the nations find their hope"* (Mt 12:21).

- *"Lord, we found him casting out demons in your name . . . No one who performs a miracle in my name will find it easy to speak evil of me"* (Mk 9:38-39).

- *"In my name they will cast out demons . . . They will lay their hands on the sick and the sick will recover"* (Mk 16:17-18).

- *"Lord, even demons are subject to us in your name!"* (Lu 10:17).

- *"Everyone who receives him, all who believe in his name, are given power to become children of God"* (Jn 1:12).

- *"Whatever you ask in my name, I will do it . . . if you ask anything in my name, I will do it"* (Jn 14:13-14).

- *"I chose you . . . so that whatever you ask the Father in my name, he may give it to you"* (Jn 15:16).

- *"If you ask anything of the Father, he will give it to you in my name"* (Jn 16:23-24).

- *"These things are written that so may believe and may find life in his name"* (Jn 20:30-31).

- *"In the name of Jesus Christ of Nazareth, stand up and walk!"* (Ac 3:6).

- *"His name, by faith in his name, . . . has restored this man to perfect health in the presence of you all"* (Ac 3:16).

- *"By the name of Jesus Christ of Nazareth . . . this man is standing before you well"* (Ac 4:10).

- See the fear the Jewish leaders had of the name of Jesus: *"Let us warn them to speak no more to anyone in this name . . . 'We strictly charged you not to teach in his name'. . . They beat them and charged them not to speak in the name of Jesus"* (Ac 4:17-18; 5:28,40).

- *"You reach down your hand to heal the sick, and signs and wonders are wrought through the name of your holy servant, Jesus"* (Ac 4:30).

- In the early church there was evidently specific teaching about the name of Jesus; a proper understanding of the significance of his name was an important part of their message: *"They believed Philip as he preached good news about the kingdom of God and (about) the name of Jesus Christ"* (Ac 8:12).

- *"Paul said to the spirit, 'I command you in the name of Jesus Christ to come out of her.'"* (Ac 16:18).

2) Concerning those references, and others like them, notice –

Probably many times the phrase *"in the name of the Lord"* means no more than acting in the place of the Lord, or upholding his honour, maintaining his cause, or defending his gospel. Other references suggest acting as the ambassadors or personal representatives of the Lord, and therefore having the same authority as if he himself were actually present.

But other references go further, and reveal that the name of Jesus has in itself divine power, and that this power can be released by faith.

The people of Bible days vested a person's name with much greater mystical symbolism than we do. A man and his name were intimately united, and each took on the other's character. That concept led the early church to believe that when they spoke in the name of Jesus they brought into the situation all the authority and power of Christ himself. Jesus and his name were inseparable. Hence we are told that

- *"his name, through faith in his name"* wrought a mighty miracle;

- Philip taught the Samaritans things *"about the name of Jesus Christ"*

- the disciples rejoiced because the demons had to submit beneath the impact of that mighty name

- it was *"through"* or *"by the use of"* his name that evil spirits were driven out

- Peter insisted that a cripple had been healed, and even the dead raised, *"by the name of Jesus"*

- and the disciples prayed that miracles might be wrought *"by his name"*.

3) Those ideas are confirmed by such statements as –

- *"God has raised Christ far above every name that is named"* (Ep 1:20-21).

- *"God has highly exalted him, and bestowed upon him the name that is above every name, so that at the name of Jesus every knee should bow, whether in heaven, on earth, or under the earth. Likewise, every tongue will confess that Jesus Christ is Lord, to the glory of God the Father"* (Ph 2:9-11).

- *"The name he has obtained is more excellent than that of any angel"* (He 1:4).

- *"This is what God commands, that we should believe in the name of his Son Jesus Christ"* (1 Jn 3:23).

- *"You held fast to my name, and you did not deny my faith"* (Re 2:13).

4) We may infer that there is great need for the church to ponder afresh *"the things concerning the name of Jesus"*, and so re-learn the splendid truth that his name, through faith in his name, can cause astonishing signs and wonders, and loose many who are captive to Satan.

CHAPTER TWELVE:

HEALING IN THE CHURCH

To long for that which comes not.
To lie a-bed and sleep not.
To serve well and please not.
To have a horse that goes not.
To have a man obeys not.
To lie in jail and hope not.
To be sick and recover not.
To lose one's way and know not.
To wait at door and enter not,
And to have a friend we trust not:
Are ten such spites as hell hath not. [25]

Indeed, to be "sick and recover not" is akin to hell on earth and hell to come. It behoves the church to take an active role in human recovery from disease. Happily, the New Testament letters (those manuals of church life) contain some striking references to the healing covenant. Christians are firmly encouraged to trust Christ as their Great Physician. This chapter will study some of these references.

A MAN DELIVERED TO SATAN

Incest was being tolerated in the church at Corinth, and Paul commanded the elders to put the wicked person out of their fellowship (1 Co 5:2,13). Further, he said that he himself would *"deliver this man to Satan for the destruction of the flesh, that his spirit may be saved in the day of the Lord Jesus"* (vs. 5).

---

(25) John Florio (c. 1553–1625), English author and translator; <u>Nolano</u>, in *Second Frutes*, ch. 1 (1591); from the <u>Columbia Dictionary of Quotations</u>.

Commentators are generally agreed that the phrase *"destruction of the flesh"* probably refers to physical sickness, to which the man would become prey if he were expelled from the church (cp. Ac 5:1-10; 13:10-11).

If disease can result from expulsion from the church, it follows that fellowship with the church confers either protection from sickness or at least a potential healing by God. Later on, when the guilty man had shown tearful repentance, Paul urged the church to forgive and restore him, which brought him back again under the protection of the covenant (2 Co 2:5-11).

THE TABLE OF THE LORD

Many of the people in the church at Corinth were sick, some had died because of disease, and the whole church was greatly distressed about the tragedy (1 Co 11:27-32). It seemed as though God's promise of healing had failed. In bewilderment they asked Paul what could be wrong.

THE CAUSE OF THEIR SICKNESS

Paul's words suggest that some kind of plague had ravaged the Corinthian church: *"Many of you are weak and ill, and some have died"* (vs. 30). Was the plague a mindless natural disaster, or did it have some deeper significance? Paul thought the plague was no mere accident. He asserted that the Corinthians were afflicted because they had come to the Lord's Table, that is, were participating in the Eucharist, in an *"unworthy manner"*. *"That is why you are sick,"* he declared.

Can that passage be taken at face value? Is it still relevant today? How could it not be? And it shows there is a reason why Christians are sick. It also shows that sickness among the people of God brings weakness to the church itself. Disease is antagonistic to God's true desire for his church.

Notice that neither the Corinthians nor Paul were eager to accept disease as the will of God. On the contrary, they were convinced that the continuing illness, and the premature death, of their fellow Christians pointed to some violation of the will of God! To them sickness was a curse, not a blessing. It was a bad thing about which they bitterly complained, not a good thing for which they praised God. They knew there must be a cause behind the onset of plague, and that cause lay in them, not in God.

But the Corinthians were unable to identify the cause. They asked Paul to show them the reason for their sufferings. His reply was succinct: they were eating and drinking at the Lord's Table unworthily. Hence, instead of gaining rich blessing and strength from their remembrance of Christ, they were *"eating and drinking judgment upon themselves"*.

But what made them unworthy celebrants?

The answer is found in one sentence: they were failing *to discern the Lord's body* (vs. 29). What does that mean? Simply that there was a breakdown in their relationship both to the mystical body of Christ, and to his physical body.

THE MYSTICAL BODY OF CHRIST MUST BE DISCARDED

    a)   The Church – the Body of Christ

The church, the universal body of believers, is described as *"the body of Christ"* – we are the *"members"* of this body, and Christ himself is the *"head"* (Ro 12:4-5; 1 Co 12:12,13,27; Ep 1:22-23; 4:12-13; Cl 1:24; 2:19).

The basic idea behind that analogy is the unity of all true believers in Christ. But if there is strife and division in the church, this unity is broken, and suffering will result (1 Co 12:26).

In the church at Corinth there was tragic disunity. The people were split into opposing parties, there was little love between the rich and the poor, little recognition of their common membership in the body of Christ (1 Co 11:13; 11:17-18,21-22).

If the limbs of a living body are torn apart, then the body will be grievously injured, perhaps destroyed. If my hands refuse to lift food to my mouth, or if my jaws refuse to chew and my mouth to swallow, then not only those parts will suffer, but my whole body will sicken and eventually die. The health of the entire body depends on the harmonious cooperation of all its members.

Likewise, if there is contention in the church, if the people are working against rather than with each other, it will lay the whole church open to disease.

Christ himself emphasised the need for us to make peace with our brother before we presume to stand before the altar (Mt 5:23-24; 18:15-

17). Again, we are told to mark those who cause division in the church, and to have no dealings with them (Ro 16:17-18). It is mandatory for every Christian who comes to the Lord's Table to come without malice, greed, envy, anger, pride, and to break bread with humility before God and with sincere love for the brethren. To fail in this is to be accounted guilty of profaning the body and blood of the Lord (vs. 27); and the cross, instead of providing mercy, may then lay us under the judgment of God.

b)   Bonded together in love

We can fail to discern the mystical body of Christ not only by wrongful participation at the Lord's Table, but also by being continually absent. We fulfil our Christian duty only when we remain an active part of the body of Christ and continue to minister to that body.

For example, your hand has no value independent of your body. Cut off your hand and it will die. A hand can thrive only as it continues to be part of a body and exists to serve that body.

Similarly, if we try to exist apart from the church we deny the purpose for which God has redeemed us, we become empty husks, withered branches, our life will moulder. We can abide in Christ, and thrive, only as we remain in dynamic union with his "body", which is the church (cp. Jn 15:1-6).

Christ gave a specific command to his disciples to break bread regularly in remembrance of him (Lu 22:15-20; 1 Co 11:23-26). The early church diligently kept his command (Ac. 2:42,46), and they reaped from their observance a magnificent harvest: *"Dread gripped everybody; and many miracles and signs were done through the apostles . . . while the Lord kept on daily adding to their number those who were being saved"* (vs. 43,47).

If the modern church does not experience such a flow of divine life, it may well be because too many of its members are indifferent to the injunction to fellowship with gladness and praise around the Lord's Table.

We are solemnly warned against *"neglecting to meet together"* (He 10:24-25), because we have an urgent responsibility as Christians and as members of the body of Christ –

- to meet together regularly in worship and in the fellowship of the church (Ps 27:4; 84:4,10; 122:1).

- to exhort, encourage, and provoke one another to good works – which itself can be done only as we regularly assemble together (He 3:13; 10:24; Ep 4:11-12).

   c)   A holy table

The awesome seriousness of these matters is shown in the following references –

- *1 Corinthians 20:21-22*. If we try to eat both at the Lord's Table and at "the table of demons" we shall provoke the Lord to jealousy; and he is stronger than we!

- *1 Corinthians 11:17*. It is possible for Christians to come together *"not for the better but for the worse"*! What an arresting saying! Church can be the most dangerous place on earth. Some people would do better to worship at a pagan shrine, or to go and play golf, than to come into the house of God. They would run less risk of incurring God's wrath!

It is a great fallacy to imagine that if attendance at church is not doing you any good at least it will not do you any harm. Rather, if you do not come to church for the *better* it may be for the *worse*. If it is not doing you *good*, it may actually do you *harm*. Some of the Corinthians discovered to their bitter hurt, and even death, that they would have been wiser not to have gone into the church at all. Their position as Christians had become more perilous than if they had remained heathens.

- *1 Corinthians 11:27*. It is a dreadful thing to profane the body and blood of the Lord. It is as though you had murdered your neighbour's child, and then sat down at his table demanding a meal. It is as though you had dragged the mutilated corpse of Jesus before the Father and flaunted his dear form before God's face. God cannot hold those guiltless who so abuse his grace (He 10:29-31).

- *Jude 12-13*. Those who violate the *"love-feast"* of Christ are reckoned already *"twice dead . . . for whom the vile dark underworld has been reserved for ever."*

I do not mean that every person who uses the Table of Christ improperly will be destroyed without remedy, nor that the Corinthians who had died in the epidemic had perished without hope. The references just quoted speak of the ultimate penalty that may be exacted from those who stubbornly despise the word and will of God; but it does not follow that such a severe penalty will always be inflicted. In the case of the deceased Corinthians, Paul's use of the expression *"sleep"* (koimaomai) instead of the harsher *"death"* (thanatos) indicates they were still numbered among the children of God. Physical death had fallen on them, but perhaps not spiritual.

Be sure to notice that the focal point of these warnings is not so much the *table* as the *body*. The Corinthians were condemned for failing to discern the *body* of Christ, not for failing to understand the *table* of Christ. The Lord's Table is a demonstration of our attitude toward the church; it is a symbol by which we express our relationship with the church. If a person is kept from the table by circumstance, or illness, or some other factor beyond his control, it will not be to his hurt, so long as he continues to *"discern the body of Christ"*.

THE PHYSICAL BODY OF CHRIST MUST BE DISCERNED

Whenever we break bread around the Lord's Table, we should –

a) recognise that his body was broken on the cross to achieve atonement for your sins and that you must, as you eat, determine to be rid of sin

- if we wilfully harbour sin, and do not repent of it, and do not wish to be rid of it, we may indeed become *"guilty of the body and blood of the Lord"*, and may *"eat and drink only to incur punishment."*.

b) *"eat worthily"* – that is, in a worthy manner, with reverence, worship, humility, praise, sincerity, repentance, thanksgiving, and love

- let no one take the bread or the cup carelessly, indifferently, or apathetically; rather, all our attention and faith should be centred on the Lord.

c) recognise that *"by his wounds we have been healed"* (1 Pe 2:24), and therefore we should firmly claim healing as we eat the bread.

Thus we *"discern"* that the body of Jesus was broken on the cross so that we might be made whole: *"he took our infirmities and bore our diseases"*.

The word *"discern"* means literally *"to thoroughly separate"*, *"to see the difference between objects"*, *"to perceive value or meaning"*. In connection with the Lord's Table it means to grasp the real significance of Jesus' broken body, to separate the meaning of his body and his blood, to understand the pardoning power of the cup, and the healing power of the bread – especially when they are taken by faith. His blood was shed for the remission of our sin, his body was broken to secure our healing. As we eat and drink at the Lord's Table we should discern these separate facts and by faith actively lay hold of God's full salvation.

WHAT WE SHOULD DO

Seeing then that we are members of the church, the body of Christ, we should make certain that

- we assemble regularly to worship the Lord and to take communion together; and that

- when we do so, that we fully examine ourselves (1 Co 11:28), so that we eat and drink in a worthy manner; and that

- we *"judge"* ourselves (1 Co 11:31) by deeply repenting of all sin, and by claiming the cleansing of the blood of Christ; and that, as we eat and drink,

- we discern the Lord's body and the healing power of Calvary, and so claim deliverance from all sickness.

If we do those things, holding firm in faith, we will not be weak and sickly as many were at Corinth, but we will be able to receive the life, strength, and health of Christ himself.

GIFTS OF HEALING

APPOINTED BY THE SPIRIT

Paul wrote about the work of the Holy Spirit in the church –

There is a variety of spiritual gifts, but only one Spirit . . . Each person who is given some manifestation of the Spirit should exercise it for the common good . . . (including) gifts of healing . . . It is God himself who has placed in the church . . . workers of miracles, then healers . . . (1 Co 12:4,7-10,18,28).

What an extraordinary passage! What a supernatural church! It contains these three powerful ideas –1)The Holy Spirit brings to the church nine supernatural gifts (or manifestations), of which two are named *"the working of miracles"* and *"the gifts of healing"*.

2) These gifts are given for the *"profit"* of the whole church. That is, they are bestowed for our benefit. But if we gain benefit from their manifestation, then we suffer loss if they are not manifested. If divine healing is *profitable* then it must be inferred that disease is *detrimental*.

SET IN THE CHURCH

1) These gifts of healing were not temporary manifestations that were soon to die out. Their permanency is shown by the following –

a) They are coupled with other spiritual gifts, such as faith, a word of knowledge, a word of wisdom. Who would dare to say that the church has no need of those? But if those other manifestations of the Holy Spirit are still valid, then it is reasonable to suppose that they are *all* valid, including the *gifts of healing.*

b) *"God has appointed"* this ministry of healing in the church. The Greek word means to *"ordain"*, *"to establish as a permanent and necessary part."* It is used of all the ministries of the church (1 Co 12:28). Just as apostles, pastors, teachers, helps, governments, and so on, have been established in the church, so have the gifts of healing. Are pastors and teachers still needed? Are they still active in the church? Then the gifts of healing should also be in continual operation – along with all the other gifts and ministries mentioned by Paul. Only unbelief has prevented the Holy Spirit from bestowing today all the gifts that were common in the early church.

2) These gifts are placed in the church in the same manner as the various members are placed in our human bodies (vs. 18). Which leads to the following –

- it cannot be disputed that we are built just the same as people were in the days of Paul, nor that just as God set the members in their bodies, so he has set the same members in our bodies.

- just as God designed and built the human body, with all its *natural* endowments, so also he designed and built the church with all its *supernatural* endowments.

- if it is still valid to liken the structure of the church to that of the human body (and it surely is), then the endowments of the church today should be as unchanged as those of our bodies – if that is not so, then Paul's argument becomes invalid.

- bodily members that are not exercised will wither away – likewise, many of these spiritual gifts have atrophied because unbelief has prevented their use; but the Lord will quickly restore them if we stir ourselves up to covet them earnestly (vs. 31).

CHAPTER THIRTEEN:

PAUL'S THORN IN THE FLESH

One Goodness ruleth by its single will

All things that are, and have been, and shall be;

Itself abiding , knowing naught of change.

This is true health, this is the blessed life.

Here, O ye prisoners of empty hope,

Minds kept in bonds by pleasure, haste ye to return.

Here, here your rest, sure rest for all your hurt,

Eternal harbour for your quiet anchorage,

Shelter and refuge for unhappy men

That's always open. [26]

Paul speaks about a *"thorn in the flesh"* that caused him much distress (2 Co 12:7-9). Linking this with other references (e.g. 1 Co 2:3-4; 2 Co 10:10; Ga 4:13-15; 6:11) it has been supposed that Paul suffered from a chronic eye disease, which rendered him nearly blind, made him weak and feeble in physical build, and gave him a repulsive appearance. That supposition has often been used as an argument against belief in divine healing. But note –

THE MESSENGER OF SATAN

1) Whatever this thorn was, it was given to Paul for a unique reason (*"because of an abundance of revelations"*) and to prevent him from becoming puffed up with pride. Paul was a remarkable man; he stands apart from all others in his personal experience with Christ (see Ac 9:1-20; 2 Co 12:1-7; Ga 1:11-24; Ep 3:1-6; 1 Ti 1:16). In other words, his

---

(26) Alcuin of York (735-804); The Oxford Book of Prayer, ed. George Appleton; Oxford University Press, Oxford, 1985; pg. 56.

example in this matter is applicable only to a person who can claim a similar degree of spiritual insight. People should not talk about God sending them a "thorn" unless they can also claim that he has carried them into a third heaven of revelation!

2)   The phrase *"thorn in the flesh"* occurs elsewhere in scripture, but not in reference to sickness. It refers, rather, to persecution and trouble (Nu 33:55; Js 23:23; Jg 2:3; 8:7; Ez 28:24; Ho 2:6). The most valid assumption is that the phrase carries the same meaning here, which is strongly confirmed by Paul's own description of the nature of the "thorn"–

a)   He describes it as *"the messenger of Satan sent to harass me"*. The Greek word for *"messenger"* occurs nearly 190 times in the New Testament. Seven times (including our text) it is translated *"messenger"*, and in each of those instances (apart from the text) it means a human messenger sent on some task. Every other occurrence of the word is rendered *"angel"*, and this is probably its sense here: *"the messenger (or angel) of Satan"*.

b)   This *"messenger of Satan"* was himself Paul's *"thorn in the flesh"*, and he brought upon the great apostle many *"infirmities"* (2 Co 12:9). Now, were those infirmities sickness and disease? They could have been, if Paul himself had not provided a detailed description of his troubles, and thus removed all doubt. Not what he says in the very next verse (10) –

> *For the sake of Christ, then, I am content with bodily frailty, insults, distress, violence, and dire hardship; for when I am weak, then I am strong.*

See also the graphic description Paul gives of his trials and sufferings in the previous chapter (11:18-30; plus 4:17-18; 6:3-5,10; etc). Who but Satan's angel could be responsible for all those sufferings? Paul mentions everything *but* sickness or sore eyes!

c) Paul said that his thorn was the messenger of Satan *"harassing"* him. The same word occurs in *Matthew 26:67; Mark 14:65; 1 Corinthians 4:11; 1 Peter 2:20*. In each of those places its meaning is self-evident, that is, an outside blow – but not sickness or disease.

It is impossible to believe that a feeble, diseased, almost blind man, could have accomplished the immense labors or endured the tremendous sufferings of Paul. He said he had labored more abundantly than all the other apostles! (1 Co 15:10). Furthermore, he often earned his own keep as a tent maker (Ac 18:1-3), an occupation that presumably required a keen pair of eyes!

PAUL AT CORINTH

See *1 Corinthians 2:3-4*. Paul's statement that he preached in Corinth in *"weakness and in deep anxiety and trembling"* cannot reasonably be construed to mean that he was sick, especially when he says in the next verse that he *"came with a demonstration of the Spirit and power"*. That is, he exercised the gifts of the Holy Spirit and displayed the power of God to heal (2 Co 12:12; and cp. Ro 15:19).

A better inference from the passage is that Paul arrived in Corinth wearied from his great exertions, both physically and nervously. He was possibly also downcast by his recent failure at Athens (Ac 17:16-34). But his *faith* was not hindered, nor the mighty working of the Holy Spirit through him. The record of Paul's labors in Corinth is not one of a sick man – see *Acts 18:1-18*.

We have already seen how Paul's ministry abounded in signs and wonders, and great numbers of healing miracles. But how could he possibly inspire others to have faith in Christ as Healer if he himself were weak, sickly, and almost blind?

Further, those who reckon Paul's thorn was sickness do so hoping to discredit the healing ministry; they want to say it is not always God's will to heal the sick. But Paul's thorn (whatever it was) had no such negative effect on him. Quite the contrary; he brought the healing power of Christ to hundreds of people!

Most people who call their sickness a *"thorn in the flesh"*, are (quite unlike Paul) sadly incapacitated by it. They are unable to *"labor more abundantly"* for the Lord; and far from helping others to have faith for healing, as Paul did, their disease may well be a discredit to the gospel and a denial of the promise of God.

Our conclusion then must be this: whatever was the real nature of Paul's thorn in the flesh, it obviously did not hinder Paul from bringing healing to those who were sick and diseased; nor did it hinder the faith people had in Christ, the Great Physician. Why then should this "thorn" be used today to destroy faith and to break down the ministry of healing?

In the next reference (2 Co 10:10), these words are found: *"his bodily presence is unimpressive and his speech is contemptible"* – from which it has been suggested that Paul was physically feeble, and afflicted by some speech impediment.

Notice, however, that those were the words of Paul's enemies. Paul himself rebutted the insulting statement. He insisted, far from being weak and contemptible, that his bodily presence would prove to be equally as forceful and moving as his letters (vs. 11). And the claim that Paul was a poor speaker and that he was physically infirm is ridiculous when placed against the record of his achievements in the book of Acts!

PAUL IN GALATIA

PAUL'S "BODILY AILMENT"

1) An eye infection?

The third passage (Ga 4:13-15) appears at first sight to prove that Paul was sick, probably suffering from an affliction in his eyes: *"You know it was because of a bodily ailment that I preached the gospel to you at first; and though my condition was a trial to you, you did not scorn or despise me . . . For I bear you witness that, if possible, you would have plucked out your eyes and given them to me"* (RSV).

That is more like a paraphrase than a translation, particularly in the use of *"bodily ailment"* and *"condition"*. The Greek passage reads literally: *"You know that through weakness of the flesh I preached."*

    a) Paul's strenuous labor

The first point to resolve is the question, did Paul preach in Galatia because of or in conjunction with *"weakness in his flesh"*. The Greek text is open to both translations.

Those (like the RSV) who adopt the first translation, assume that a sudden attack of sickness compelled Paul to change his plans and to remain in Galatia to convalesce. *"Because of a bodily ailment"* he found himself obliged to stay there, and so was able to preach to them.

Those who adopt the second translation, prefer to read the phrase as *"amid bodily weakness"*, or *"through infirmity of the flesh"* – the idea being that Paul preached in Galatia amid many troubles and difficulties. In other words, "the infirmity of which Paul speaks was not the cause of his preaching, but rather the accompanying circumstances."

If it was sickness that made Paul stay at Galatia, there is no indication of it in the record of his first visit to that area, nor in the record of his second and third visits – see *Acts 13:14-14:25; 16:1-6; 18:22-23*. On the contrary, Luke talks only about Paul's immense efforts to spread the gospel, with many instances of the supernatural power of God confirming the message he preached (e.g. Ac 14:3; Ro 15:18-19).

b) "Ailment" or "weakness"?

The Greek word translated as *"ailment"* can mean sickness, but it can also mean just weakness – cp. *1 Corinthians 2:3; 2 Corinthians 13:4; Hebrews 11:34*, where the same word is used. It can refer to just the kind of weakness caused by the many difficulties Paul suffered on his first visit to Galatia (Ac 13:45,50-51; 14:2,4-5,11-14,19).

That is surely the proper meaning of the word in this place. Confirmation is found in the next phrase, *"the trial that was in my flesh"*. Because of variations in the Greek text, there is a difference of opinion here: should the statement be taken to mean *Paul's* trial or the *Galatians'*! Was Paul's *"weakness"* a trial to him, or to them? Probably it was a trial to both!

c) But was it sickness?

The word translated *"trial"* is used twenty other times in the NT, and not once does it obviously refer to sickness. Its natural meaning is temptation, putting to the proof, calamity, especially in the sense of any kind of outward trouble, adversity, or spiritual temptation. It could include illness, but that would be unusual.

In any case, the word should here be given its ordinary meaning of adversity. The facts of Paul's life surely preclude disease. We are not told anywhere in Acts that he was delayed in Galatia because of sickness;

but we are told about the tumult of persecution, slander, and peril that was associated with Paul's hectic missionary journeys. Significantly, his suffering was especially acute during his first period in Galatia. As William Hendriksen remarks

> These experiences were never erased from (Paul's) memory. Even in his very last epistle that has been preserved the afflictions suffered on that journey march in rapid procession before his mind's eye, as he writes to Timothy: "You, however, followed my . . . persecutions, my sufferings, what kind of things happened to me at Antioch, at Iconium (and) at Lystra, what kind of persecutions I underwent; yet from them all the Lord rescued me! (2 Ti 3:10-11). [27]

Martin Luther is quite emphatic on the matter –

> The first benefit (saith Paul) . . . was this: "When I began first to preach the gospel among you, and that through the infirmity of the flesh and great temptations, my cross did nothing at all offend you" . . . This is indeed a great commendation of the Galatians, that they received the gospel of a man so contemptible and afflicted on every side as Paul was . . . For all the mighty, wise, religious and learned men, hated, persecuted and blasphemed Paul . . . (but) the Galatians were no wit offended, but (turned) their eyes from the beholding of this infirmity, these temptations and dangers . . . Jerome and certain other of the ancient fathers expound this infirmity of the flesh in Paul, to be some disease of the body, or some temptation of lust . . . (but) Paul calleth the infirmity of the flesh no disease of the body or temptation of lust, but his suffering and affliction which he sustained in his body . . . As though he would say: "When I preached the gospel among you I was oppressed with sundry evils and afflictions; I was always in danger both of the Jews and

---

(27) New Testament Commentary, "Galatians", pg. 171; Baker Book House, Michigan, 1974.

of the Gentiles, and also of false brethren; I suffered hunger and wanted all things; I was the very filth and off-scouring of the world." He maketh mention of this his infirmity in many places, as in 1 Corinthians 4; 2 Corinthians 4;6;11;12; and in many other. [28]

This public opposition to Paul, and the infamous notoriety he had gained, would dispose most citizens to despise and shun him. But because of the signs and wonders wrought by his hand, at least some of the Galatians ignored his public reputation and received him as an angel of God (cp. Ac 14:8-13). Indeed, they loved him so well, that when he was flogged and stoned and driven out of their towns they risked the ire of the authorities to minister to him. In fact, they would have gladly *"plucked out their eyes"* to help him (Ga 4:14-15).

There is no reason to suppose that graphic phrase means Paul was afflicted in his eyes. He is no longer talking about his *"infirmity"* in this verse, and the saying probably means no more than our own expression, "I would cut off my right arm to help him!" It was simply a pungent way of describing their desire to aid Paul.

2) No longer present

Paul uses the past tense when he reminds the Galatians about his bodily *"infirmity"*. Whatever it was, whether an ailment or outward persecution, it was with him only on the occasion of his first visit to Galatia (vs. 13). It was not present with him during his subsequent visits nor at the time he wrote them.

My claim that the *"infirmity"* was not sickness, but the severe persecution and trouble Paul suffered in Galatia, is confirmed by the facts here. Although he did suffer many indignities on his first visit to the area, his following two visits were free of any such trials (Ac 16:1-6; 18:22-23) –

- Paul's enemies were completely silenced, and he traveled freely and preached openly (in the Galatian district) so that *"the*

---

(28) <u>Commentary on Galatians</u>; James Clarke & Co. Ltd., London, 1956; pg. 399-401.

churches were built up in faith, and their numbers grew daily" (Ac 16:5).

- Paul *"went from place to place through the region of Galatia and Phyrgia, encouraging all the disciples"* (Ac 18:23).

Neither of those descriptions seems possible if Paul was weakened by disease and nearly blind!

PAUL'S STRANGE WRITING

The final verse is *Galatians 6:11*. One well known commentator says it clearly shows Paul was suffering from acute opthalmia, to the point of almost total blindness. That is the reason, it is claimed, why Paul usually dictated his letters to an amanuensis (see the postscript added to Paul's letters in most translations). However (say these commentators), Paul had no secretary at hand when he wrote to the Galatians; hence he was compelled to write the letter himself, with great difficulty, penning large scrawly letters because of his near blindness.

The Greek sentence readily lends itself to two different translations –

- either, *"See how large a letter I am writing to you with my own hand;"* or,

- *"See with what large letters I am writing to you with my own hand."*

Commentators and translators seem to be equally divided between the two. What shall we say then? Was Paul talking about his big *letter*, or his big *letters*?

1) Paul's "big letter"?

The first translation simply means that Paul, either by choice or because he lacked an amanuensis, penned the entire letter himself instead of just the few closing lines (as was his usual custom; see, for example, 1 Co 16:21-24, plus postscript; Cl 4:18, plus postscript; 2 Th 3:17-18, plus postscript). Several authorities confirm this view –

> The apostle . . . as a particular mark of his respect for
> them, had written this large letter with his own hand, and
> had not made use of another (Matthew Henry).

(The phrase means) "how large a letter". . . this (letter) is called long, because it was on one subject, by the hand of Paul himself, on a point on which the Galatians should have been long ago established . . . He had not heretofore written a longer epistle (J. A. Bengel).

(Paul) means to refer to the size of the epistle which he had written . . . (This) is, indeed, the common interpretation, as it is the obvious one. According to this, it was proof of special interest in them, and regard for them, that he had written to them a whole letter with his own hand (Albert Barnes).

You see how many things in a letter I have written to you with my own hand (Diaglott).

"Behold," saith Paul, "what a letter I have written unto you with mine own hand." This he saith to move them, and to show his motherly affection towards them. As if he should say: "I never wrote so long an epistle with mine own hand to any other church as I have done unto you." (Martin Luther).

That is the traditional view, and if it is correct, there is obviously no thought of partial blindness behind Paul's words.

2) Paul's "big letters"?

Some translators prefer the alternative rendering: *"See with what large letters I am writing"* (RSV); *"Look with what huge letters I am writing"* (Hendriksen); *"I will write these closing words in my own handwriting. See how large I have to make the letters"* (Taylor); *"You see these big letters?"* (NEB).

But does even that translation (as Taylor seems to indicate) mean Paul had diseased eyes? Hardly! It could just as readily mean he was unaccustomed to writing in Greek, hence his ordinary use of an amanuensis. It was not uncommon in those days for quite well educated men to be unskilled in the mechanics of writing. The task of writing was often left in the hands of slaves or professional scribes. Paul may have written Hebrew with ease, but perhaps not Greek.

Another suggestion is that Paul wrote only the closing verses of the letter himself (vs. 11-18), and that he wrote in large letters as a means of deliberate emphasis. Several authorities support this –

> "Look at these huge letters I am making in writing these words to you with my own hand." According to centuries-old Eastern usage, this could easily mean, "Note how heavily I have pressed upon the pen in writing this." Thus it could be translated, "Notice how heavily I have underlined these words to you." (J. B. Phillips).

> "Mark carefully these closing words of mine. See with what large letters I am writing them with my own hand" (Amplified NT).

> "I conclude in my own handwriting – mark in what bold emphatic characters I have set it down" (Way).

> "In how large letters" – the reference is to the size of the characters, in which he wrote the passage from vs. 12 to the end, just as we now print in large characters what is peculiarly important. (Heinrich Meyer).

So the meaning seems clear. Paul may have written the whole letter in his own hand, and then drawn their attention to it; or he may have written only the last portion, emphasised with large letters (in the same way that many important statements in these notes are written in italics). But in either case, his intention was not to make a whimsical remark about the size of his writing, caused by his supposed darkened vision, but to compel the readers to take special note of the vital matters he had set down.

To go beyond that is mere supposition; to suggest that Paul was almost blind over a period of many years – the years of his most ardent labors – lacks any firm support either in scripture or logic.

CHAPTER FOURTEEN:

SOME SICK PASTORS

Hey nonny no!
Men are fools that wish to die!
Is 't not fine to dance and sing
When the bells of death do ring?
Is 't not fine to swim in wine,
And turn upon the toe,
And sing hey nonny no!
When the winds blow and the seas flow?
Hey nonny no! [29]

W ho but we Christians can turn "the bells of death" into a merry dancing tune? Who but we have such a hope in Christ that we know we shall never die? (Jn 11:26). Yet what is sickness but incipient death, and what is each miracle of healing but a foretaste of the coming resurrection? If I can believe that Christ can (and will) raise my dead body from its grave, how should it be difficult to trust him to raise my sick body from its bed? Yet there are some who scorn the healing covenant on the ground that three early church leaders suffered illness –

EPAPHRODITUS

This faithful servant of God became ill and was *"near to death . . . because of his work for Christ."* He *"risked his life"* to serve Paul on behalf of the Philippian church (Ph 2:25-30). The cause of his illness seems to have been unsparing labor in ministry, a physical collapse due to over work. But the church, and Paul, prayed for him, and *"God had*

---

(29) Anonymous 16th century song.

mercy on him." He was soon fully recovered and Paul was able to send him back to Philippi with a letter.

So Epaphroditus is an example of the healing ministry at work in the church, and also that healing was not always instantaneous; it sometimes took the form of gradual recovery.

Epaphroditus may also be taken as an illustration of sickness resulting from breaking the laws of God – whether his moral law or physical law. In this instance God's physical law was violated. Our bodies are *"the temples of the Holy Spirit"*, and we are commanded to care for them, and by them to bring glory to God (1 Co 6:19-20; 3:17-18). Accordingly we are under obligation to give our bodies all due care, proper nourishment, and rest, along with our work and play.

Despite the short time of his public ministry and the tremendous need of the multitudes who thronged him, even the Lord Jesus Christ frequently drew aside, either by himself or with his disciples, for times of rest and refreshing (see for example Mt 14:13,23; Mk 6:31; 7:24; Lu 9:10).

TIMOTHY

Paul advised Timothy, *"No longer drink only water, but take a little wine to ease your stomach and prevent your frequent ailments"* (1 Ti 5:23).

Apparently Timothy lacked a strong constitution and was prone to constant stomach upsets. His infirmities were obviously not serious – else he could not have fulfilled his arduous duties as general overseer of a number of churches – but they were sufficient to be troublesome. The particular cause of his trouble lay in the water he was drinking. Even today, with our clean water supply, people are frequently made ill by the local water when they move from one town to another. In the ancient world the problem was vastly more acute.

Timothy was a conscientious young man, and had apparently refused to drink any wine (cp. 3:3), preferring to suffer from the effects of the unsafe water. But Paul urged him to be more sensible, to stop drinking water only, and to drink a little wine instead – at least until he had fully recovered and was able to drink the water without distress.

No doubt, as often as he took sick, Timothy had sought God for healing. But there was a lesson to be learned: it is foolish to expect healing from God while continuing the cause of the sickness!

We are expected to use good sense and wisdom in our approach to the promises of God.

Note also: the promise of divine healing does not usually include a change in our physical nature and build. Some are born healthy, strong, and vigorous. Others have different dispositions. Our bodies are still *"mortal and corruptible"* and will not become truly immortal or wholly incorruptible until the day of resurrection (1 Co 15:51-54). Until that day, whether we have a build that is weak or strong, we can certainly claim healing from God if disease catches us; but we must also sensibly avoid things that have an ill effect on us.

TROPHIMUS

Opponents of the ministry of healing triumphantly cite this man as a clear example of it not being always God's will to heal. Paul, they say, left Trophimus at Miletus because he was unable to heal him (2 Ti 4:20). But let us not be too hasty! Other things may be said –

- Healing is not always instantaneous. The promise of God is only *"they shall recover"*. No doubt Paul had prayed for Trophimus, and possibly he was soon fully restored; but at the time Paul left the city, he was still sick.

- If Trophimus failed to recover it could have been his own lack of faith. The Lord Jesus Christ left many sick people at Nazareth, and he left a multitude of infirm and diseased people at Bethesda (Mk 6:5; Jn 5:3,13), but this did not prove the failure of his healing ministry nor that he was unwilling to heal them.

- Trophimus may have been afflicted because he had *"failed to discern the Lord's body"*, in which case not even the most fervent apostolic prayers could help him, because recovery lay in his own repentance and discernment (1 Co 11:30-32).

- He may have been guilty of sin, and so could not find healing until he had repented, confessed his fault, and sought the prayers of the elders (Ja 5:14-16).

- He may, like Epaphroditus, have exhausted himself, and so suffered a physical and nervous breakdown; in which case healing could only come by rest and slow restoration of health and strength.

- He may have been old and so come to the end of life's journey, for there is a time appointed for each one of us to die.

- He may, like Timothy, have been suffering merely from some physical infirmity or upset, which nature itself would cure in process of time and which did not need the intervention of divine power.

Any of those reasons, and others like them, could explain the case of Trophimus. But one thing is certain: surely it is folly to quote this one example against the mass of other biblical testimony in favor of divine healing for all!

PAUL'S GREAT PRAYER

May the God of peace himself sanctify you wholly and may your spirit and soul and body be kept sound and blameless at the coming of our Lord Jesus Christ (1 Th 5:23-24, RSV).

The Greek word translated *"sound"* is the same word Peter used when he said that faith in the name of Jesus had brought *"perfect soundness"* to a formerly helpless cripple (Ac 3:16). The word (holokleros) means *"whole, having all its parts sound, perfect, complete in every part."* It is a vivid and expressive word, and it gives us a graphic insight into the tremendous scope of the message Paul proclaimed. His was no mean faith!

The apostle's deepest wish for the saints at Thessalonica, and presumably for us also, encompassed healing in every part of their lives, spiritually, mentally, physically. Paul wanted them to be radiant with health, strong and vigorous, so that when they drew their last breath their lives might be accounted blameless. He obviously believed the gospel gave people an opportunity to be set free from every bondage and to be made perfectly well. He saw that Christ had died to make it possible for men and women to have minds that are clean and free, bodies that are healthy and vigorous, and spirits that are untainted by guilt or shame! That is a great deliverance indeed, a marvellous promise – may our faith be equal to it!

THE CHASTENING OF THE FATHER

See *Hebrews 12:3-13*. The chief emphasis of this passage is how to cope with persecution, trouble, and difficulty (vs. 3-4). However, the example of Job, and Paul's instructions to the Corinthians (1 Co 11:29-32), show there are occasions when God may cause (or allow) his children to be afflicted with sickness, as a means of divine discipline.

Paul told the people at Corinth that they were being chastened by plague, which suggests that disease may well be included in the process of discipline spoken of in *Hebrews*. But the apostle also told the Corinthians, if they would judge themselves, and properly discern the Lord's body, then the hand of God's judgment upon them would be lifted.

The same is implied in *Hebrews*. The writer indicates that the chastening of the Lord will continue only as long as needful. Far from meekly resigning themselves to illness, the Hebrew Christians were urged, *"lift your flagging hands, straighten your trembling knees, and stop treading a wavering path; then your crippled limbs will no longer fall out of joint, but instead will be healed"* (vs. 12-13 and cp. Is 35:1-10).

When he quoted that passage from *Isaiah*, the writer to the Hebrews probably intended to convey a symbolic rather than a literal sense. But if it happens that the Lord chooses illness as a method of chastisement, then the literal sense of the words would be quite applicable. This is confirmed by the original prophecy. Isaiah was clearly describing the mighty salvation and deliverance the Lord would bring his people in the latter days –

> *Say to those whose hearts are fearful, "Be strong and no longer afraid! Behold, your God is coming to take revenge by punishing iniquity; but to you he brings salvation." Then the eyes of the blind will be opened, and the ears of the deaf unstopped. Those who are lame will leap like young fawns, and those who were dumb shall sing for joy . . . And all whom the Lord has ransomed will (be given) joy and laughter, and sadness and sighing will be banished for ever.*

Christ himself plainly had that passage in mind when he used its words to describe his own healing ministry (Lu 7:21-22). He evidently accepted that the words of the prophet could be taken quite literally. They promised divine healing to the ransomed of the Lord, which hopefully, dear reader, includes you.

CHAPTER FIFTEEN:

A BETTER COVENANT

THY restless feet now cannot go
For us and our eternal good,
As they were ever wont. What though
They swim, alas! in their own flood?

Thy hands to give Thou canst not lift,
Yet will Thy hand still giving be;
It gives, but O, itself's the gift!
It gives tho' bound, tho' bound 'tis free! [30]

P aul was adamant in his confidence: if God was willing for our sake to give his only Son to unsparing pain and death, how much more must he be willing to give us all subordinate gifts! (Ro 8:32) Surely the lesser is contained in that which is so vastly superior? Christ himself is the greatest possible gift, alongside whom all other prizes shrink to littleness. Thus the life he offers overwhelms all that belongs to death. Bodily healing becomes just a fragment of that greater substance, the first surge of the coming resurrection, the beginning of our ultimate total and endless victory over sin and death.

A similar idea is expressed by the apostle in *Hebrews*. Thirteen times he uses word *"better"* to contrast the old covenant given through Moses with the new covenant given through Christ. The Greek word is *kreisson* = "more excellent, more useful, of a higher nature, more effective"; it is

(30) Richard Crashaw. 1613?–1649; <u>Christ Crucified</u>; The Oxford Book of English Verse, 1919 edition.

found in *Hebrews 1:4; 6:9; 7:7,19,22; 8:6* (twice)*; 9:23; 10:34; 11:16,35,40; 12:24.* One passage in particular stands out –

> *Christ has obtained a ministry which is as much more excellent than the old as the covenant he mediates is better, since it is enacted on better promises (8:6, RSV).*

In connection with the healing ministry, two statements in that verse are especially significant –

A BETTER COVENANT – A BETTER PROMISE

WE HAVE A BETTER COVENANT

The covenant established by Christ surpasses that of Moses because it is

- acceptable to all people and not just to one nation
- based upon more excellent principles [31]
- centred on a heavenly kingdom, not an earthly empire
- concerned with eternity as well as time
- the reality that fills up the shadows and types of the past.

WE HAVE BETTER PROMISES

There were, as we have already seen, many great promises given to Israel in conjunction with the Mosaic covenant. [32] But the promises found in the gospel of Christ are *"better"*.

Now that is a simple word, and its meaning is clear. It leads us irresistibly to say that the gospel, when it is compared with the old covenant, offers:

- a *better* pardon
- a *better* honour
- a *better* answer to prayer
- a *better* eternal home

---

(31) That is, upon love instead of fear, faith instead of law, grace instead of merit, divine suffering instead of human sacrifices, and mercy instead of judgment.

(32) See the volume that precedes this one, "Healing in the Whole Bible – Old Testament."

- a *better* hope
- a *better* life
- a *better* deliverance
- and so on.

In short, whatever the Old Testament offered has been bettered by the gospel of Christ. The goodness of the old is vastly exceeded by the new. It brings us greater advantages, it removes the burdens of the law, its terms are more easily accepted, it promises total security.

With regard to bodily healing, it would seem reasonable to understand *"better"* to mean that the gospel contains a promise of healing that is superior to the promise of old. I cannot accept that God would "improve" the old covenant by supplanting its promise of bodily healing with one saying that the best he can now do is to give us grace to bear suffering patiently!

The Bible was written in the language of ordinary people and its words carry the meaning they have in ordinary speech. If that were not so, the writers of scripture would be guilty of extraordinary duplicity! A word on the pages of the Bible usually means the same as it does on the pages of a dictionary. Thus, "better" means: "improved", "more advantageous", "good qualities increased", "surpass", "outdo", and so on. And with regard to sickness, it surely means recovery and health: for do we not say that a sick person who has recovered is "better"?

If the old way included freedom from sickness (and we saw earlier that it did) then the new and better way in Christ must contain an even stronger promise of health, an even greater security from disease, and an even more powerful method of healing.

CALL FOR THE ELDERS

See *James 5:11,13-18.*

Those verses deal with the matter of sick people in the church. They are found in a letter widely recognised as the first of the New Testament letters, written before any other. James was a brother of the Lord, an apostle, and one of the chief leaders of the early church (Ga 1:19; 2:9; Ac 21:18). Being written by such a man, and addressed to the large number of Jewish Christians who had been scattered abroad by persecution (Ja 1:1-3), and who were in urgent need of guidance and instruction, this earliest of the letters has special interest and value. It is particularly significant that among the fundamental instructions he set down, James included guidance on what Christians should do in sickness.

Concerning this important passage, note . . .

PRAYER OR THE PHYSICIAN?

The Bible contains instruction on every aspect of life – the home, marriage, business attitudes, eating and drinking, pleasure, worship, how we should dress, citizenship, personal relationships, family life, and so on. Would it not be remarkable if no specific guidance had been given to the church on a matter of such prominence as illness? As it happens, James provides us with plain and forthright instruction. It is strange to find Christians who always consult God's Word for advice in every other situation of life, yet fail to seek his wisdom in the matter of sickness!

But there *is* a problem! We cannot fail to notice an absence of all references to drugs or doctors. How shall we interpret this singular lack, which was shared by Paul? Notice that he too failed to suggest that people who were diseased (even when they were dying) should seek medical help. Instead, he told them (the Corinthians, for example) to repent and properly discern the Lord's body. Likewise, when Epaphroditus was close to death, and when Trophimus was sick at Miletus, Paul sought the mercy of God on their behalf.

Does this mean that we should disparage medicine? Should we forbid Christians to have recourse to a physician? That would be foolish indeed! Given the primitive state of medicine in those days, it is hardly surprising that people would try almost any remedy before, despairingly, they turned to the doctors (cp. Lu 8:43 [33]).

---

(33) Note that across twelve years she had *"spent all the money she possessed on doctors"*, but to no avail. It is surprising to read this humble admission of inadequacy by Luke, who was himself a physician. Yet it was perhaps not so surprising when you learn about the techniques used in those days. Here are some that I have read about in various places –

♦ compel the patient to drink a foul brew made from weeds (on the premise, one supposes, that the worse it tasted the better it must be)

Footnote continued on next page.

Nonetheless, we cannot be sure, even if medical science had been highly advanced in those days, that the apostles would have urged people to consult their physician. But we *can* say this: the command to call for the elders of the church *cannot be held to include a prohibition against calling for a doctor.* The command does no more than show where a Christian should place priority. Those who belong to the church of Jesus Christ should *first* direct their prayer to the Lord, and only then, if necessary, seek the physician. But a great many people, even Christians, are like Asa of old: *in sickness they forget God and turn only to their doctor.* They credit God with no power to heal, they have no confidence in his ability to hear their cry for recovery.

However, lest I should be misunderstood, let me clearly affirm that medical skills, like all other human abilities, are God's gifts to man, and we are free to use them for God's glory. Doctors are very necessary in many circumstances – for example, when sudden surgery may be needed, in childbirth, when accidental injury occurs. The Lord Jesus Christ spoke well of the Good Samaritan in this connection (Lu 10:35-37). We are

---

- bind the sick with ropes into a magical crouching posture, and leave them to suffer hours of agony

- take the ashes of an ostrich egg and bind them around your waist with a fine linen cloth (a remedy that only the fabulously wealthy could afford

- brew and drink a mixture of wine, rubber, alum, and crocus flowers; or, if that proves impossible to find or to swallow, try a mixture of wine and onions

- push patients off a high cliff into the ocean below, where orderlies in a row-boat are waiting to fish them out – a kind of primitive shock treatment

- feed barley corn to a pure white donkey, pick the partly digested corn out of the animal's dung, and then feed it to the patient

- for poisoning, sew the victim into the warm carcase of a newly disembowelled calf, showing only his or her head, and leave the sufferer there until death or a cure results

- for a spotted and infected face, hang the patient by the neck until almost dead, and then lance the infected pustules

- to cure cancer, eat your own excrement

- to cure headaches (a remedy that pre-dates Moses), drill two or three holes into the sufferer's head, so that the demons can escape!

---

also enjoined to conform to the laws of the land, and should therefore be obedient to any health ordinances that are laid down, or to any medical requirements that may reasonably be demanded of us (cp. Ro 13:1-5; Tit 3:1; 1 Pe 2:13-17).

The wise Christian will try to avoid the two extremes of depending only on human ability without God, or of depending only on God without doing anything to help himself.

In the matter of sickness, those extremes are observed in people who depend only on the physician, leaving no place for divine healing; and in people who depend only on prayer, leaving no place for medicine.

A more balanced approach is to pray first, placing the matter in God's hands, and then to take whatever human remedies may be available. If I may speak personally, here is the approach that my wife and I follow for our family in times of serious illness –

- we first seek guidance from God as to how we should handle the situation

- sometimes God gives us faith to pray for and receive a clear miracle of healing, without the aid of physician or potion

- otherwise we deem it wise to seek all the help medical science can offer

- but at all times we seek to obey the command given by James, to offer a prayer of faith, and to expect that good health will be restored to us or to our loved ones.

With that background, let us look more carefully at the instruction James gives –

CALL FOR THE ELDERS

The apostle claims the attention of sick people in the church with the words: *"Is anyone among you sick?"* So he is about to give advice to the sick. What will he say? Meekly accept and patiently endure your affliction? Turn at once to a physician and freely use every drug he prescribes? Hardly! His advice, inspired by the Holy Spirit, is plain, and obligatory for all who accept scripture as their rule of life: those who are sick are instructed to call for the elders of the church – whether before or after calling for a physician must presumably depend upon the circumstances.

The purpose behind calling for the elders of the church is to receive healing as a direct answer to prayer; and the implication is surely that prayer *may* be effective without interposing medicine. How can it be surprising that many people have never experienced a direct miracle of answered prayer when they have never allowed God the opportunity to do so?

This, then, is certainly the natural and primary meaning of the instruction: the sick person should call for the elders in expectation that prayer alone will bring healing. However, it cannot be inferred that such will always or necessarily be the case. James' silence on the addition of medicine to the prayers of the elders cannot be construed as teaching that God must heal independently of medicine or not at all.

The passage teaches rather that in sickness the prayer of faith should be offered for healing, whether or not the sick person resorts to the physician. God *may* heal in answer to prayer alone, and prayer should be the first resort of all afflicted persons; but the Lord may just as readily choose to heal through the use of natural means.

Logically, only those Christians who actually believe in the healing covenant can properly turn to medicine when they are sick. Those who believe sickness is the will of God should surely accept it humbly, take no steps to cure it, but leave it wholly to God to choose if and when they should recover!

For my part, since I believe that God has made a covenant of healing with me, I feel myself free to make use of any available means to promote good health.

The wisdom of Christians calling first for the elders of the church (unless the nature of the ailment demands immediate medical attention) is confirmed by the possible occurrence of sickness as divine discipline. In such cases it may be futile to seek physical healing until the spiritual or moral causes of the affliction have been removed. In any case, can bodily health retain any final value when the soul is sick? Only the elders of the church are in a position to aid sick people in such matters.

It follows from this, if the sick are to call for the elders of the church, then those elders must be willing to come and pray for the sick person.

They must be consecrated people, men and women [34] of faith and spiritual authority, who know the promises of God and the healing power of Christ: such people alone should be recognised as true elders.

The elders have a responsibility, not to pray *"for"* the sick person, at a distance, but to go to him or her and pray *"over"* the sufferer. In that way a personal contact of faith is made, and the elders display the compassion of Christ. The phrase *"pray over the sick person"* implies an aggressive confronting of sickness in the authority of Christ; it requires an attitude of faith that reckons itself master of the worst of Satan's oppressions.

The elders are then commanded to anoint the sick person with oil, as a symbol of the presence of the Holy Spirit, and a sign of consecration to God's service. "Oil" in the scriptures usually signifies these things: surrender to God's will; dedication to his purpose; and the power and unction of the Holy Spirit. To the elders, the oil is a sign of the power of God manifested in them as they lay hands on the sick person and pray. To the sick person, the oil depicts his need to consecrate himself anew to God's service when his health is recovered. [35]

---

(34) If you baulk at the idea of female elders, which many people do with great sincerity, then simply omit the reference to "women" and construe instead an all-male eldership.

(35) I regard as hardly worthy of comment, the suggestion that oil was used as a primitive form of universal medical treatment, although that idea has been put forward by some quite reputable scholars. For example, H. H. Halley: "Anointing with oil was a recognised medical treatment (Is 1:6; Lu 10:34) to be reinforced by prayer, not to be used for magical purposes." And K. S. Wuest claims that the Greek word translated anoint (*aleipho*) is used of greasing machinery, of giving the body an olive oil massage, of greasing a harness to prevent chafing, and of application of oil "for medicinal and remedial purposes in the case of illness . . . we see this use of the word in Mk 6:13 and Ja 5:14. Thus we find in the latter text the two God-appointed resources in the case of illness, prayer and medical help . . . "

Wuest actually translates the passage: *" . . . let them pray over him, having massaged him with olive oil in the name of the Lord . . . "*

Footnote continued on next page.

"The prayer of faith will save the sick man" (KJV)

The word "save" is *sozo*, which means (as I have shown above) deliverance, healing, restoration, of both body and soul, a complete recovery of the whole person.

This recovery is dependent upon the elders and the sufferer uniting together in *"a prayer of faith"*. That is, they are required to pray with assurance, expecting God to answer with a gift of healing. And that assurance should be maintained, even if there is no immediate sign of recovery. (See Mk 11:24; 1 Jn 5:14-15, noting especially *"believe that you receive it"*, and *"we know that we have obtained the requests made of him"* – and that *"believing"* and *"knowing"* must be steadfastly maintained until the cure is effected – He 10:23; 11:1; 10:36-38).

However, there is a tension here (as there is in other places in scripture) between *our* appropriation of the promise and the sovereignty of *God*. It is true that our normal approach to the healing covenant should be one of bold faith and vigorous application of the promise to our personal need. If the healing covenant is to have a continual and effective outworking in the church then it must be approached with that kind of confidence.

Yet withal, there are times when faith must surrender before a manifest act of divine sovereignty. To cite an obvious example: if the prayers of the elders were always effective, without exception, then none of us would ever die, except perhaps of sudden accident. The existence of death precludes the healing promise from being absolute. As strong as the promise is, there is another word that is stronger: *"It is appointed unto humans once to die."* And this appointment with death is not always

My response to those gentlemen is to suggest in their case the proverb needs to be rephrased: "Too much knowledge is a dangerous thing." They have allowed their great erudition to run away with their common sense. Apart from the fact that any Greek Lexicon will show that aleipho had a wide variety of applications, both secular and sacred, it is absurd to suppose that James and his friends believed in oil as a cure for every sickness. Even in those days, and despite the primitive state of medical science, people had access to a wide variety of medicines for many different ailments. It is foolish to imagine the early church completely ignoring the doctors that were available and calling the elders instead to administer medical treatment. In fact, they called the elders to do only what they were qualified to do, namely, pray. If medical care were needed, they would have sensibly called for a physician.

reserved for the aged – not all the prayers of all the elders in Israel could have saved the life of David's infant son (2 Sa 12:15-23).

So we must concede that there are times when it may not lie within the immediate purpose of God to allow healing to come, or when the decree of God is death (remember though, *"Precious in the sight of the Lord is the death of his saints,"* [36] Ps 116:15). When such cases occur, it must be hoped that the church is sufficiently attuned to the Holy Spirit to discern them (as Elihu so nearly discerned the purpose of God for Job). Otherwise it is proper for the church to take an aggressive stand against sickness, and to pray for and expect a steady flow of the miracle-working power of God.

So I am saying that the presence of death and the presence of a higher divine purpose preclude the promise from being taken as absolute. Yet in practice (as indicated by the bold words of James) the church should proceed as though the promise were in fact absolute. Until the contrary is shown, the injunction should be acted on with confidence: *"the prayer of faith will save/heal the sick person, and the Lord will raise him up!"*

Notice that the word *"if"* in the next clause (*"if he is guilty of sin he will be forgiven"*) indicates sometimes illness may result directly from sin, but not always.

In a general sense, of course, every sick person is indeed a sinner, as we all are; but the supposition here is that this sickness is related to a particular sin, so that the sufferer needs special pardon as well as healing. The same clause also shows that James was using *sozo* ("save") in the sense of physical healing rather than spiritual salvation – but both ideas are included, as he showed by adding a specific promise of pardon.

Sometimes when *sozo* is used, the idea of physical healing is more prominent; at other times the spiritual aspect is to the fore; and sometimes both ideas are equally important.

---

(36) The nature of death, the present state of the dead, the resurrection, the judgments of God, are discussed in my book on the return of Christ, <u>When the Trumpet Sounds</u>, and also in <u>The Cross and the Crown</u>.

James enlarges on that last point by indicating that the illness, if caused by sin, may not be cured unless the sick person repents – *"confess your sins to each other, and pray for each other, so that you may be healed."*

But what *"sins"* is he talking about? Is James encouraging the vicious and reprehensible practice of baring to the gaze of other people every moral and spiritual obliquity of which the sick person is guilty? That would be inconceivable! He does not instruct the sufferer to confess every fault to the elders. Rather, his meaning is evidently restricted to an offense or injury caused to some other person.

Ordinarily we need confess our sins only to the Lord to find full pardon and release (1 Jn 1:9:2-2). But if in our sin we have offended or harmed a particular person (especially another Christian), we should seek that person's forgiveness before we come to the Lord (cp. Mt 5:23-24; Mk 11:25-26). The principle violated here is that of failing to discern the Lord's body (1 Co 11:28-33).

To encourage faith in the promise, and patience in faith, James reminds the people of Job. Not only of Job's patience, with which most people are familiar, but also of what most people forget: *"the purpose of the Lord, how the Lord is compassionate and merciful"* (Ja 5:11).

There are many of the saints of God who are afflicted with some chronic illness, who think of themselves as fellow-sufferers with Job. They remember the first part of James' advice (*"we call those happy who are steadfast"*) and they are trying to emulate the patience of Job (*"you have heard how steadfast Job was"*). But they forget that God's real purpose for Job, the real end of his compassion and mercy, was found in a mighty miracle of pardon and healing, along with a restoration of the patriarch's abounding prosperity!

By all means let us remain patient while we await the outworking of God's will; but above all, let our anticipation, if we are sick, remain steady that God will display the same compassion and mercy toward us and grant us the same great miracle of healing!

Finally, to encourage faith in this ministry of healing, James quotes the example of Elijah (vs. 17-18), who teaches us that the *"prayer of a righteous person is mightily powerful and effectual!"*

CHAPTER SIXTEEN:

LIFE, LOVE, AND MANY DAYS!

"In times gone past, all who turned their faces toward the Brass Serpent were healed; not by the object they gazed upon, but by Thee, the Saviour of all. That is how our enemies were persuaded that You can well deliver Your people from every evil. Our enemies were unable to find any cure for their misery, so they died from the sting of the locust and the hornet . . . but Your children did not succumb . . . because you came to their aid, and in Your mercy You healed them. . . . No herb or poultice could make them well, O Lord, but only your glorious Word, for you alone hold the power of life and death" (Wis 16:6-13). [37]

See *1 Peter 3:7-13*, where the apostle insists that you have been called *"to obtain a blessing, and to love life, and to enjoy prosperous days."* But how can this be true if one is racked by fever and pain? Our days become then times of affliction and suffering, and of sorrowful prayer. Only the merry can truly sing praise to God (cp. Ja 5:13). Yet Peter is confident: the ordinary will of God for his people is a joyous, healthy, love-filled life, rich in divine benefits.

There are exceptions, of course. The promise is not absolute – as Peter himself admits when he prepares his readers for the possibility of being called upon to suffer for Christ (vs. 13-17). But times of persecution and other special exceptions aside, we may usually pray for and expect a life filled with blessing. Yet there are some conditions attached to the promise –

---

(37) From the OT Apocrypha, <u>The Wisdom of Solomon</u> is a pseudonymous work, composed perhaps around 100 B.C., and reckoned to stand among the best of the ancient Jewish "wisdom" writings.

- husbands must honour their wives, lest their prayers be hindered (vs. 7)

- we must have love and compassion for each other for we are members together of the body of Christ (vs. 8)

- we should desire each other's welfare and happiness, knowing we have all been called to receive the Lord's blessing (vs. 9)

- we must refrain our lips from speaking deviously (vs. 10)

- we must do good and follow after peace with God, our neighbor, and within ourselves (vs. 11)."

- *"For the eyes of the Lord are upon the righteous and his ears are open to their prayer"* (vs. 12).

Those who live in conformity with God's standard in those things can expect to have a life filled with love and with the daily goodness of the Lord.

MORE REASONS TO BELIEVE

Once belief in the healing covenant has been established, many other NT references will then seem to embrace the same great promise. Here are some of them –

GOD'S MIGHTY PROMISES

Once again the apostle Peter takes up his pen and triumphantly declares that

> *(God's) divine power has provided us with everything that belongs to life and godliness . . . (He has also) given us his precious and very great promises, so that by them you may shake off all the corruption that belongs to the world. (2 Pe 1:3-4).*

While the primary idea in that passage may be escape from moral and spiritual corruption, we also reasonably infer that *"everything that belongs to life"* and *"escape from the corruption that is in the world"* (RSV) include physical life and healing. Indeed God *has* given us everything we need for life – eternal life in the future and a more abundant life right now (Jn 10:10). Whatever we need to live to the full extent of our capacity, to realise all the potential God has built into each one of us, physically, mentally and spiritually, is available to us in Christ.

The channels of this divine grace are the *"precious and very great promises of God"*. To those who receive the promise, who understand it, who vigorously appropriate it by faith (Mt 11:12) – to them is opened a channel through which the mighty power of God can flow to deliver them from all the corruption that is in the world.

The *"word"* has always been the vehicle by which the power of God has travailed to do its perfect work – he created all things by his word (He 11:3), he upholds all things by *"the word of his power"* (1:3, lit; that is, the word through which his power flows), and he challenges us (as he challenged Abraham) to have an aggressive and unwavering confidence in that word (Ro 4:19-21).

PROSPERITY AND HEALTH

See *3 John 2*.

Earlier we considered the great prayer of the apostle Paul, that men and women might be made whole in their entire body, soul and spirit. Here we have a similar prayer offered by the beloved disciple John. He prayed that *"in every respect"* (lit.) his friend Gaius might prosper and be in health. This prayer, coming as it does from the disciple who knew Jesus most intimately and who was deeply loved by Jesus, may be fairly taken, not just as John's wish, but as the actual desire of God for his people.

PROSPERITY

John prayed, *"I ask that all go well with you,"* or, *"I ask that you may prosper in every possible way."* The Greek word for *"prosper"* means literally "to help along the way". Paul used the same word when he prayed that he might have *"a prosperous journey"* to Rome. From this idea of safe and enjoyable travel the word came to mean success in achieving any goal. So John was expressing his belief that God wants to help each of us reach our proper goal in life. We should never doubt it! The Lord wants to bring you and me along the road to success; he wants to give us the desires of our hearts; he wants to answer our prayers; he wants you and me to *prosper*!

HEALTH

John prayed, *"May you be in health!"* Can there be any reasonable doubt that he means *physical health*? This prayer shows John's confidence that God's wish is for his children to enjoy good health. There may, we must allow, be extraordinary circumstances where the contrary becomes true, or where spiritual well-being must take precedence over bodily health. But ordinarily those who love the Lord may assume that he wants them to be free from sickness.

SOUL

There was a basis upon which John built his prayer for Gaius. It was this: *"I know that it is well with your soul."* Because the apostle knew that his friend was *spiritually* healthy, therefore he was able to pray audaciously that God would prosper him *materially* and *physically*. The lesson is obvious.

VARIOUS OTHER REFERENCES

Matthew 6:25-34. If we need food and clothing for life, we also need good health. When I was the father of small children, I was not content to give them just enough to eat and to wear, merely to keep them alive. I so fed and clothed them that they should be healthy, strong, and happy. Can I doubt that my heavenly Father cares for *me* the same way?

John 15:5-7. There is no sickness in the Vine, neither should there be any in the branches. If illness does occur, the Lord's promise is emphatic: *"Ask what you will, and it will be done!"* Added to that promise, of course, are all the other invitations Christ gave, to ask for whatever we desire (see Mt 7:7-8; 21:21-22; Mk 11:22-24; Jn 14:12-14; 15:16; 16:23-24; etc.)

1 Corinthians 6:13,20. My body is *"for"* the Lord; that is, it must be devoted to God's service, to his honour and glory, to the fulfillment of his will. But then, God is *"for"* my body; that is, he is willing to act on behalf of my body, to meet its needs, to prosper it, to promote its well-being. It does not seem unreasonable to include physical healing in that undertaking.

Galatians 1:8-9. If we are to preach the same gospel Paul preached, without alteration, addition, or subtraction, then our gospel must include divine healing.

Ephesians 1:19-22. *"God's immeasurably great power"* is working in us now (if we release it by faith, vs. 18), to bring us daily victory over sin, mastery over Satan, health, strength, and freedom.

Philippians 4:13,19. Since a sick person needs and wants health in the same way that a hungry person needs and wants food, this promise may be taken to include divine healing.

Colossians 1:27; 2:10. If Christ, the Author of life, truly dwells in us, and if we are truly *"complete in him"* (filled with all the fulness of God), then we ought to rise up in faith and take hold of these tremendous resources. Thus the glory of Christ will be released within us to bring life, strength, and health.

Hebrews 4:15-16. If Christ feels our every infirmity, then let us flee to him who is filled with such compassion, who is willing to meet our every need.

HEALING IN PROPHECY

History shows that belief in the healing power of God never became wholly extinct in the church. In every generation there have been some who clearly saw the divine promises and who laid hold of them by faith. Over the centuries the faith of the church in the healing covenant has waxed and waned, but the covenant itself has remained unchanged. Furthermore, the scriptures make it plain that the promise is continuous with the Christian era; therefore until Christ comes and the new age begins the promise will remain valid.

THE PROPHECY OF JOEL

See *Joel 2:28-32.* Peter quoted this prophecy in his sermon on the day of Pentecost (Ac 2:16-21), but it is plain from the original context that its fulfilment did no more than *begin* on that day. Its promise obviously spans the entire Christian era, right until the day of Christ's return.

The prophecy predicts a continuous outpouring of the Holy Spirit and a continuous offer of *"deliverance"* to all who call upon the name of the Lord. The early Christians understood those words to include a mighty display of the supernatural power of God, channelled through the extraordinary gifts of the Holy Spirit, which include *"gifts of healing"* (1 Co 12:7-11).

There is no justification for limiting the prophecy to a prediction of *spiritual* salvation, without any offer of *physical* healing. If the *"spiritual"* aspect of the prophecy is still valid, then its *"physical"* must be equally valid. In other words, the prophecy entitles the church today to expect the same flow of divine healing that the early church experienced.

FALSE CHRISTS AND FALSE SIGNS

See *Matthew 7:21-23;* and cp. *24:4-5, 11, 24-25; Mark 13:5-6,21-23; Luke 21:8.*

Those references cannot strike against genuine miracles of healing wrought by the power of the Holy Spirit; but that has not prevented opponents of the healing ministry from using them to prove that anyone who practices divine healing must be a false prophet.

But who were those people described by Christ, who claimed to be servants of God, yet were rejected by the Lord? They cried out, *"Lord, Lord, did we not prophesy in your name, and cast out demons in your name, and work many miracles in your name?"* But he rejected them: *"I never knew you; get away from me you frauds!"*

The following suggestions can be offered –

1)   This claim of miracles wrought in Christ's name was theirs, not his. It is possible they had done nothing of the sort; therefore he refutes their claim and banishes them.

2)   However, it is more probable that the things they described had actually happened; in which case there are several possibilities –

a)   Despite the use of Jesus' name, these miracles may have been wrought by demonic power, or by the use of cunning magic (cp. the magicians of Pharaoh, who matched their own prodigies against those of Moses).

b)   Despite a religious covering, these "miracles" may have stemmed from the use of psychosomatic or auto-suggestive techniques that were antagonistic to Christian values.

c)   The people claiming these miracles may have belonged to semi-Christian cults, of which there are a number, which use Christian terminology, but so distort the gospel that they have no genuine claim to be recognised as Christian. Yet there is often a spiritual vitality in such groups by which some amazing things occur.

d) In the gracious providence of God, the persons concerned may have been permitted to exercise a Christian ministry, even to perform *"mighty works"* when all the time their hearts were far removed from him. Judas, for example, preached, healed the sick, and cast out demons alongside the other disciples, while never truly yielding himself to Christ in loyalty and love. He was always spawn of Satan.

3) Whatever the nature of the miracles wrought by these people, one thing is certain: they were not wayward or backslidden Christians; they never *were* Christians. At no time had they deserved to be recognised as children of God. They had always been strangers to Christ. Their profession of his name was spurious, outward, artificial. His rejection of them will be emphatic: *"I never knew you; get away from me!"*

So those people will be condemned, not because of the miracles they will claim (whether or not they were genuine), but because of a *character* failure. Yet it is interesting to notice something else that Christ was showing. In the coming crisis of judgment, when spurious ministers are frantically seeking entrance into paradise, they will claim three things: *prophecy, exorcisms,* and *miracles.* Clearly, they will make this claim because they suppose that those three things will have great weight with Christ. Some would argue that any claim based upon outward signs instead of inward spirituality has already revealed the claimant's true nature: worldly, superficial, opposed to Christ. But Jesus did not dispute either the propriety or the validity of the claim; he merely asserted that he did not know the persons concerned.

Since Christ himself originated this account, and since the scene is intended to span the entire Christian era, the inference is strong: there are three things the church should be able to claim, right up until the end of the age. Those three things, which should everywhere and always be part of its ministry in the name of Jesus, are *prophecy, miracles of healing,* and *mighty works.* Those powerful tools were clearly intended by Christ to continue throughout the entire Christian era; if they belong only to the first generation of Christians, then his story has little relevance to later generations. Instead, Jesus portrays people, right up until the day of judgment, claiming prophecy, miracles, and healing as proof of the authenticity of their faith. Surely this strongly shows that such things were expected by Christ to remain a continuing part of the ministry of his church?

In the case of the people in our text, their demand to be welcomed into the kingdom claim will be disallowed; but that does not negate the argument. On the contrary, those whose claims are false will hardly dare to assert themselves on that day unless they observe others whose claims are genuine being approved!

HEALING IN THE MILLENNIUM

Many references depict the radiant health and happiness that will fill the earth during the millennial reign of Christ (see Is 35:5-6; 65:20-25; Ez 47:8-12; etc.)

Those prophecies undoubtedly point forward to the joyous blessing that will enrich the coming kingdom of God; but there is a sense in which the church has already entered the millennium. We are already *"seated in heavenly places with Christ . . . (and) blessed with every spiritual blessing"* (Ep 1:3,6). We have already *"tasted . . . the powers of the age to come"* (He 6:5). Figuratively and literally the blessings of the coming kingdom era are already available to us in Christ.

That idea is confirmed by the habit the NT writers have of applying to the present church prophecies that strictly belong to the age to come – e.g. *Isaiah 35:5-6* is referred to in *Luke 7:22*; *Acts 26:18*; *Matthew 11:5*; *Mk 7:37*. The number of such prophecies quoted in the NT runs into scores. If one of the outstanding characteristics of the millennial kingdom is the health and happiness of its citizens, and if the church has already entered this kingdom in spirit, then we may claim its promise of healing.

CONCLUSION

The promise will be ours tomorrow, and it is ours today –

> *He showed me the river of the water of life, sparkling like crystal, flowing from the throne of God and of the Lamb . . . also . . . the tree of life . . . whose leaves will bring healing to the nations. Never again will any accursed thing be allowed there, but the throne of God and of the Lamb will be there, and his servants shall worship him . . . Blessed are those whose robes have*

been washed clean, for they will have a right to the tree of life! . . . Let every one who is thirsty come, for anyone who yearns for it may freely take God's gift of the water of life! (Re 22:1-17).

BIBLIOGRAPHY

Believer's Bible Commentary; William Macdonald; Thomas Nelson Publishers; 1989.

Bible Background Commentary; Intervarsity Press, Nottingham UK; 1993.

Bible Days Are Here Again; by Gordon Lindsay; Gordon Lindsay Pub., Shreveport, Louisiana, 1949.

Bible Knowledge Commentary, The; by John Walvoord and Roy Zuck; Cook Communications, Colorado Springs, Colorado; 1989.

Bodily Healing And The Atonement; by T. J. McCrossan; T. J. McCrossan Pub. Seattle,Washington, 1930.

Calvin's Commentaries; John Calvin (1509-1564).

Christ The Healer; by F. F. Bosworth; Fleming H. Revell Co.,USA.1963.

Columbian Dictionary of Quotations, The; Columbia University Press; 1995.

Commentary on Ephesians, A; Charles Hodge (1797-1878).

Commentary on Galatians; James Clarke & Co. Ltd., London, 1956.

Commentary on the Bible; Adam Clarke (1715-1832).

Commentary On The Old And New Testaments, A; John Trapp (1601-1669).

Commentary on the Old and New Testaments, A; Robert Jamieson, A. R. Fausset, David Brown; 1871.

Cross and Crown, The; by Ken Chant; Vision Publishing; Ramona, California.

Essay on Criticism, An; Alexander Pope (1711).

Explanatory Notes on the Whole Bible; John Wesley (1703-1791).

Exposition of the Entire Bible; John Gill (1690-1771).

Expositor's Bible Commentary, The; ed. Frank E. Gaebelein; Zondervan Publishers, Grand Rapids, Michigan.

Expository Commentary; H.A. Ironside (1876-1951).

Faith Dynamics; by Ken Chant; Vision Publishing; Ramona, California.

Healing the Sick; by T. L. Osborne; Osborne Ministries Int., Tulsa, Oklahoma.

Healing; by Francis McNutt; Bantam Books Inc., New York, New York.

Healing Rays; by George Jeffreys; Henry E. Walter Ltd., London, Worthing, 1952.

Interpreter's Bible, The; Abingdon Press, New York; 1952.

Isaiah 53, Is There Healing In The Atonement? by Ray Hubbard; New Life Press; Bromley, Kent, 1972.

IVP New Testament Commentary Series, The; Intervarsity Press, Nottingham, UK.

Jewish New Testament Commentary; David H. Stern; Jewish New Testament Publications, Inc., Clarksville, Maryland; 1982.

Matthew Henry's Commentary; Marshall, Morgan, and Scott, London; 1953.

Matthew Poole's Commentary; 1685

Mountain Movers; by Ken Chant; Vision Publishing; Ramona, California.

New Testament Commentary; Baker's Publishing House, Grand Rapids, Michigan; 1987.

New Testament Commentary; *Galatians;* Baker Book House; Michigan; 1974.

None Of These Diseases; by S. I. McMillen; Fleming H. Revell Co., Westwood, N. J. 1963.

Notes on the Bible; Albert Barnes (1798-1870).

Oxford Book of English Verse, The; ed. By Arthur Quiller-Couch;1919.

Oxford Book of Prayer, The; ed. George Appleton; Oxford University Press; 1985.

People's New Testament, The; by B. W. Johnson; 1891.

Poor Man's Commentary On The Whole Bible, The; Robert Hawker; 1850.

Preacher's Commentary, The; Word Inc., Nashville, Tennessee; 1992.

Pulpit Commentary, The; ed. Joseph S. Exell, Henry Donald Maurice Spence-Jones; 1881.

Throne Rights; by Ken Chant; Vision Publishing; Ramona California.

Vincent's Word Studies; Marvin R. Vincent; 1886

When the Trumpet Sounds; by Ken Chant; Vision Publishing; Ramona, California.

Wiersbe's Expository Outlines; Warren W. Wiersbe; Publisher, David C. Cook, Colorado Springs, Colorado.

Word Pictures In The New Testament; A. T. Robertson; 1933.

Other Books By Ken & Alison Chant

Angelology
A study of the splendours of the heavenly realm

Attributes of Splendour

Reflections on the nature, being, and glory of God

Authenticity and Authority of the Bible

The Authenticity and Authority of scripture

Better than Revival
A Pragmatic look at Christian Ministry and the Idea of Revival

Building the Church God Wants
Not goal-setting, nor statistics, but faithfulness

Cameos of Christ
OT prophecies fulfilled in the life of Jesus

Christian Life
A positive and creative approach to life.

Clothed with Power
A Pentecostal Theology of Holy Spirit baptism.

Corinthians
Studies in 1 Corinthians

Dazzling Secrets
For Despondent Saints the causes and the cure of depression.

Demonology
Understanding and overcoming our dark enemy

Discovery
Learning and living the will of God

Dynamic Christian Foundations
Studies in Foundational Christian Truths

Emmanuel 1
Jesus: Son of Man.

Emmanuel 2
Jesus: Man who is God.

Equipped To Serve
Understanding, receiving, & using the charismata to Serve

Faith Dynamics
The limitless power of faith in God

Great Words of the Gospel
The major themes of salvation and holiness.

Healing in the New Testament
The healing covenant now.

Healing in the Old Testament
The healing covenant then.

Highly Exalted
The ascension and heavenly ministry of Christ

Mountain Movers
Secrets of mountain-moving prayer

Royal Priesthood
The priesthood of all believers.

Songs to Live By
Studies in the Psalms and Christian worship.

Strong Reasons
The Bible & Science, and the Proofs of God.

The Cross and the Crown

The passion and resurrection of Christ.

The Pentecostal Pulpit
The art of preaching in the power of the Holy Spirit.

The World's Greatest Story
The dramatic first millennium of church history

Throne Rights
Our position and spiritual authority in Christ.

Understanding Your Bible
Studies in biblical hermeneutics.

Unsung Heroines
Sage counsel for women in leadership in the church.

Walking in the Spirit
The Apostle Paul's key to successful Christian living.

When the Trumpet Sounds
Studies in the Return of Christ.

www.ingramcontent.com/pod-product-compliance
Lightning Source LLC
Chambersburg PA
CBHW051720090426
42738CB00010B/2003